RISK TO GAIN

Christmas 1998

Fritz & Lucy,

Thanks for all your support over the years! This was a great project that you had an instrumental role in for me.

Thanks and enjoy!

© PHOTOGRAPHY RICK TOMLINSON © TEXT MARK CHISNELL AND MAX STRÖM

PRODUCTION: MAX STRÖM. EDITOR: JEPPE WIKSTRÖM

DESIGN: PATRIC LEO. PRINTING: VÄSTRA AROS, VÄSTERÅS, SWEDEN, 1998. COLOUR SEPARATIONS: FÄGERBLADS, VÄSTERÅS

BINDING: BARRESJÖ BOKBINDERI, STOCKHOLM

ISBN 91-7588-226-4

RISK TO GAIN

THE DRAMATIC ACCOUNT OF TEAM EF'S WHITBREAD VICTORY - TOLD BY ANNA DROUGGE & MAGNUS OLSSON

Photography by Rick Tomlinson
Written by Mark Chisnell

CONTENTS

STOCKHOLM, SEPTEMBER 1995:

Magnus Olsson hung up the phone and sat back slowly in the chair. He had known Johan Salén for a long while and perhaps Johan had a point. Perhaps he wasn't quite ready to retire to the tranquility of Stockholm's waters. The conversation was supposed to have been about financing a Whitbread 60 as a sponsorship vehicle and for corporate team-building events. But somehow they had ended up talking about doing another Whitbread Race. Johan was keen and his enthusiasm was infectious. Magnus picked up his cup of coffee and blew gently across the top before sipping thoughtfully. Another Whitbread ...

The best and worst of times. He could remember the twenty-hour days to get Drum rebuilt after the keel fell off on the Fastnet Race, so close to the start of his first Whitbread in 1985/86. But the rock star welcomes around the world, with Simon Le Bon aboard, had made every minute worth it. In the 1989/90 Race they had collided with a spectator boat and ripped the mizzen mast out of The Card at the Auckland restart, then sailed four thousand miles through the Southern Ocean with no chance of winning. Soaring highs and crashing lows, but none quite like 1993/94, when, as watch captain aboard Intrum Justitia, he had overseen the building of the boat in England, and helped sail her to stunning wins in both the Southern Ocean legs. Then in Leg Five, Tokio's mast had come tumbling down off Brazil, handing Intrum Justitia the lead just before she entered the Doldrums. But by the time she came out the other side Yamaha had slipped past and built a margin that was impossible to break. Within a few days they had grasped victory, only to watch it turn to water and slip back through their fingers.

He could taste that feeling, breathe that short experience again now. So what would it be like to enter the Solent knowing that in just a few more miles you had won the greatest ocean race in the world? A little shiver shook him; the coffee slopped out of the cup, but Magnus barely noticed the spreading stain on the carpet at his feet. He was far away: so many miles, so many good friends and so much raw experience. And the prize at the end, the greatest rush of all? Winning, which had eluded him in three laps of the planet. But leaving Margareta and the children, Niklas and Joakim, to go back into the Southern Ocean? Should he take those risks? He and Johan had learnt a lot though, together and apart; they could do it properly this time. Johan had some ideas for the main sponsor, a company called EF Education. The owner, a man by the name of Bertil Hult, was interested in talking to them. Magnus licked some coffee off his fingers absently. There's no harm in talking, is there?

Vilamoura, Portugal, February 1997: Anna Drougge shifted uncomfortably in the leather sofa and tried to stifle a yawn. She needed a shower and something to drink. It had been a long day. Another long day in an endless sequence of long days. Anna had been with Team EF for over a year, through a spring and summer of trialling and sailing in Sweden, then on to their warm-water Portuguese winter-training camp. It had been good to leave behind the frozen seas of Sweden, good to be so close to the open ocean of the North Atlantic. But there had been so many days of practice; endless repetitions of every possible manoeuvre and eventuality, of preparing and refining the boats and equipment, testing and developing everything from the meals through the computer software to the sails.

But it would all be worth it if she could realise her dream to race the Whitbread. And Team EF, with their resources and equipment, could not only make that possible, but with the added expertise of the men they had a real chance of success. Anna glanced around at the girls with her: Leah Newbold, Marleen Cleyndert, Bridget Suckling, Keryn McMaster, Katie Pettibone and Christine Guillou. They all looked as tired as she felt.

The hotel was quiet. The waiting was beginning to get them down. There had been hundreds of applicants since it was first announced that Team EF would enter both an all-men's and an all-women's boat in the forthcoming Whitbread. Many of those who applied had come and gone, and of course some had stayed longer than others. But this little group of seven had coalesced into the core sailing team during the summer, autumn and winter. What they didn't have was confirmation of that from the Team EF management. Perhaps this was the meeting when they would get it.

But Anna didn't want to let herself think like that

– she'd been there too often before. In fact, in every meeting with the project management since November, she'd hoped that they would confirm her place on the women's crew. It had been a frustrating time – worse for Anna than for the others, since she had been with the project the longest. When EF had bought Intrum Justitia as a training boat sixteen months earlier, Anna was already working aboard her. Magnus had been managing Intrum at that time, and it had been natural that the newly formed Team EF should buy the Whitbread 60 that was in his charge as a training boat. Anna had met Magnus in Auckland during the previous Whitbread. She had been there on holiday, partly to see the finish and the restart of the race. She shared a background with Magnus in offshore yacht racing in Sweden, and they got on well.

So Anna was pleased, if a little surprised that he had remembered her, when Magnus asked her to help him deliver Intrum Justitia from Gothenburg to Stockholm the following summer. One thing led to another, as it so often does when a job is well done, and Anna was soon working on the boat full time. There was a season of racing in Sweden sponsored by Sony, and a winter of looking after the boat in Stockholm. And in that time Team EF grew and developed around her. Magnus was now a senior member of Team EF – sailing director and a watch captain aboard EF Language for his fourth Whitbread Race. But Anna was still feeling desperately uncertain.

There was the sound of footsteps on the stone floor.

'I've got some good news,' said a voice behind them.

Anna froze.

'You're all to be offered a place on the crew of EF Education.'

Anna smiled, but only briefly. It had been a long wait. The overwhelming emotion was relief, rather than triumph. She had finally been given the opportunity to join that rare band of sailors who had raced a Whitbread. Now they could really get on with the job, and show what they could do.

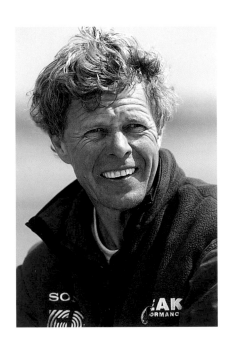

MAGNUS OLSSON

ANNA DROUGGE

NEXT PAGE: THE START OF THE 1997/98 WHITBREAD RACE IN THE SOLENT.

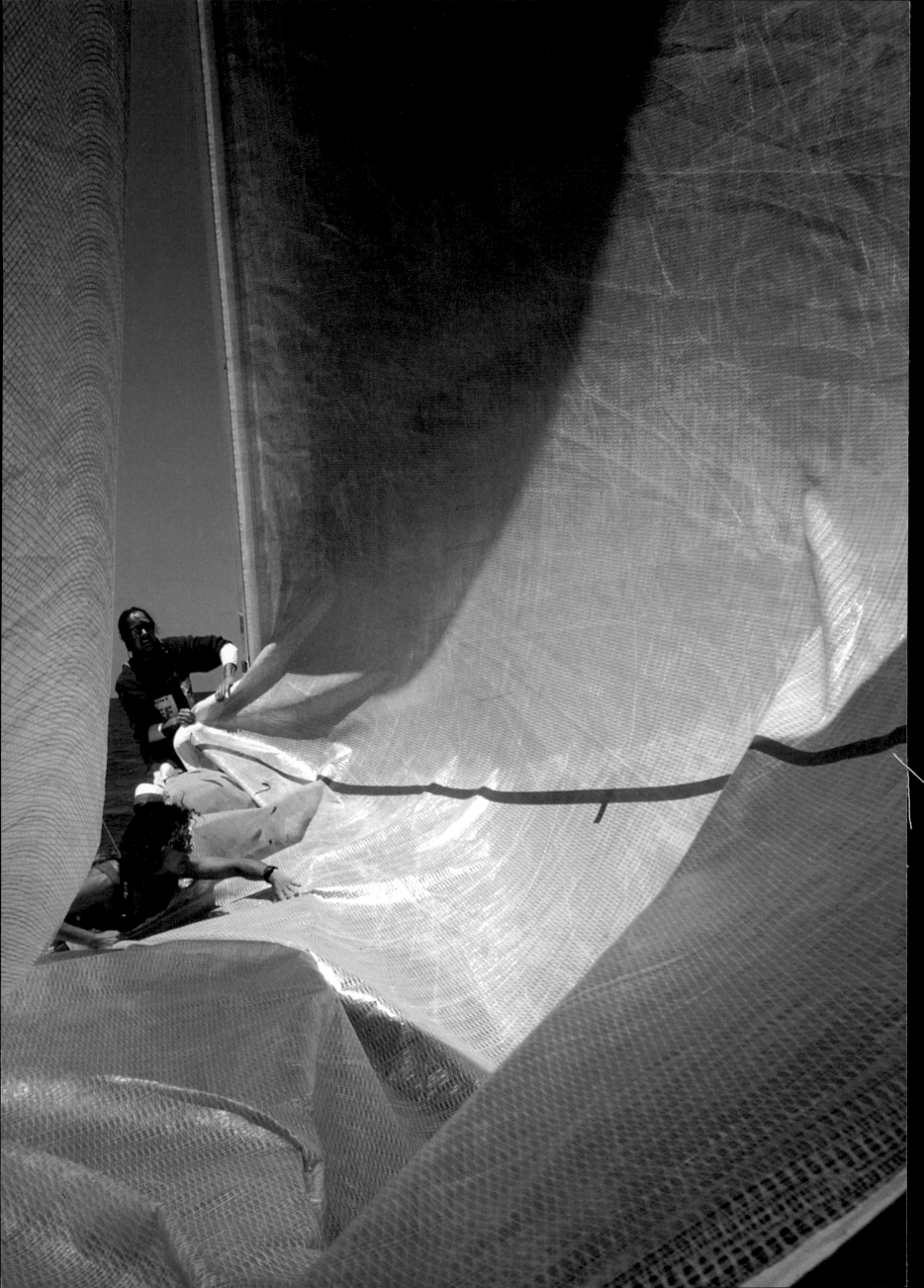

THE WATER-MAKER

13

The first and longest leg of the 1997/98 Whitbread Race, 7,350 nautical miles from Southampton to Cape Town, and things were not going well for the women aboard EF Education. They had stayed too far from the coast of France on the first morning of the race. A sea breeze developed inshore, and seven of the fleet had slipped away to a commanding lead. So far there hadn't been an opportunity to get back into contention. The weather patterns continued to favour the leaders, and EF Education trailed the fleet towards the Equator. The only consolation was that their team-mates aboard EF Language were part of the breakaway group, and held third position.

Anna:

We were all thirsty. With the temperature well into the thirties, it was hot, fry-an-egg-on-the-deck hot. The boat was thrashing along with a number two headsail, just far enough off the wind to edge up the speed. The heat was relieved on deck by the breeze, but down below it was stifling. Lying motionless in a bunk was enough to work up a sweat, minerals pouring through the skin in a constant metabolic flush. The air lay heavy, with a warm, sticky saltiness. In those conditions being thirsty is par for the course. There were no ice-cold cokes on this boat, they're too heavy. Trouble was, there was very little water left either. Leah heard it first, the disturbing rattle from under the floorboards. It was about four in the afternoon on October 6. The noise was coming from the generator and its accompanying drive shaft. Leah was convinced that it was the water ballast pump. That's powered by the generator, and it moves the water between

the boat's six ballast tanks. At least that was easy to access and check - you just pull up a couple of floorboards.

Leah gave Lisa a hand to dismantle the ballast pump and put it back together. But there was nothing obviously wrong with it, and when they restarted the generator the noise was still there. It was as loud as ever and more ominous, because the only other thing connected to that drive shaft was the water-maker pump. All the drinking water on a Whitbread 60 is made by a desalinator. A highly complex series of chemical membranes and filters, it takes in pressurised salt water from a through-hull fitting, and spews out fresh drinking water. The water is forced through the desalinator by the pump, driven from the boat's generator.

They checked the desalinator unit and, sure enough, there was no drinking water spouting from the outlet. But by then it was too dark to work any more. Lisa called off the repair efforts until dawn. As a precaution, Christine introduced water rationing: no more water for cooking, and a maximum of a litre on deck per watch. It was a strict regime, but we all knew that if we couldn't fix the water-maker, it was a long way back to the Cape Verde Islands.

The following morning Lisa took charge of the operation. As the engineer, it was her responsibility. She knew that if the water-maker system was the prob-

lem, there were two possible sources: the pump itself or the wheel and shaft driving it from the generator. The whole thing is encased between the media station and the galley, and to get to it we had to dismantle both, and then pull up the floorboards. That done, Lisa had to lie on her stomach in the bilge, one leg jammed against a strut to try to keep herself balanced against the motion of the boat. She could just get her hand through the access hatch and reach round towards the drive wheel. She could see what she was doing through the gap created by the missing floorboards – provided someone else held a torch in from above where the galley had been.

We all took turns with the torch, watching her grope and fumble, stretching and adjusting her position until she could get her hand on the drive wheel. It was loose, that's what was causing the rattling. Now Lisa didn't just have to reach the drive wheel, she had to reattach it to the drive shaft to see if that fixed the problem. The drive wheel was attached to the shaft by a tiny grub screw, which tightened through a thread cut in the wheel, down on to the shaft. The only screwdriver that would fit both the confined working space and the head of the grub screw had a short, thin handle. It was almost impossible to get a decent grip on it and apply any turning force to the screw. It would have been almost impossible if the boat had been tied to the dock. But it wasn't. It was

LIGHT AIR WAS A RESPITE AS (BELOW) LISA CHARLES BRACES
HERSELF IN THE BILGE TRYING TO REATTACH THE DRIVE WHEEL TO THE GENERATOR SHAFT.

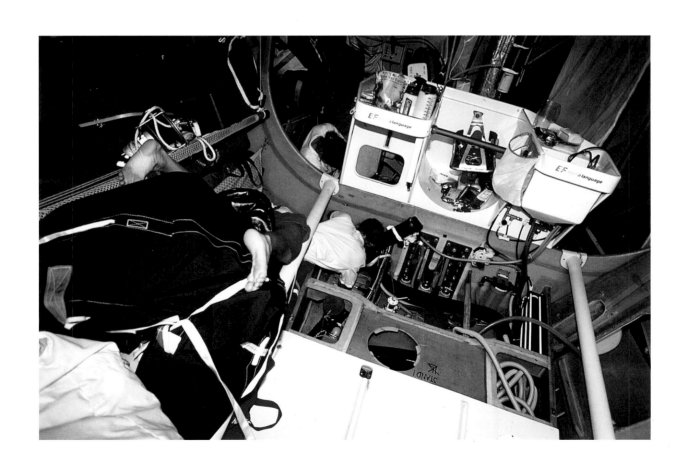

ALMOST EXHAUSTED, LISA CHARLES AND ANNA DROUGGE TRANSFER THE WATER-MAKER HOSES
TO A SPARE PUMP DRIVEN BY THE ENGINE, RATHER THAN THE GENERATOR.

fully powered up, heeling at twenty degrees and plunging through the Atlantic Ocean.

It was brutal work – and almost as bad watching with the torch. Lisa was struggling to hold herself still enough just to keep the screwdriver in place on the screw-head, never mind tighten the screw. The heat was unrelenting, the lack of water added to her growing cramp. Sweat was running into her eyes, streaming down her arms and hands. Her mouth was dry and her head spinning from being jammed into the tight space while the boat was in motion. She had almost no grip on the screwdriver. Every time it slipped off the screw-head she had to adjust her position to relocate it. Countless tiny little frustrations built up as the day wore on.

Then there were larger frustrations. If she tried a little too hard to apply some pressure, and the boat lurched over a bad wave, the screwdriver slipped from her sweaty, greasy hand into the bilge. Then it would take five minutes to find it and fish it back out. It happened once, twice, a third time – large frustrations building onto smaller ones. You could see how easy it would be just to scream out loud and pound on the deck, but that's not her style. Lisa Charles was going to wear the problem down until it gave in. And it did. She got the wheel relocated, and tightened, and ready to test. Everything seemed solid. Someone pressed the starter button and for a few seconds it ran smoothly. Then there was a clatter and the rattle returned. The biggest frustration of all – three hours' work and we'd got nowhere.

You just have to start from the beginning and try again. Two hours of sweat and frustration later Lisa was convinced that she'd got the grub screw tighter. She was wrong again. The wheel spun loose after a few revolutions. I remember watching her sit back and stare into space. I thought that she was finally going to lose it. Up on deck winches still clattered and sails were still trimmed. The boat was racing as hard as ever. But every mile we sailed, we might have to sail twice more if she couldn't fix it – and quickly. Pressure builds on the frustration, on the failure. Watches came and went, and assistants came and went with them as Lisa tried other solutions. She pulled the pump apart – thinking maybe it was seizing up and that was what was breaking the drive wheel loose. There was no oil in it, but nor did it look like there should be. She put it back together and tried again. No dice. She tried moving the drive wheel along the shaft – that didn't work because the belt was pulled out of line. Every time she wanted to test it she had to painstakingly rebuild the system. Struggling with every screw against the motion, the cramping, sweaty fingers. Every time, the same rattle, twelve hours of heartbreaking effort – for nothing.

By sunset the water rationing – a litre for each watch when we would expect to drink five or more – was really starting to hurt. Thirst and anxiety were affecting us all. Once again, however, there was nothing we could do in the dark. Work was suspended until the following morning. For the second night, there was no water for cooking dinner, but at least the temperature dropped a notch or two. That was a small relief from the hunger, the stress and the thirst. Lisa resumed work at dawn the following morning, when it was my turn to help her again. She was convinced that we couldn't repair the original pump and drive system. There was one final possibility. If that failed we would have to turn back to the Cape Verde Islands for help. We wouldn't die of thirst – there was a hand-pumped desalinator aboard that could provide enough water to get us there. But at the rate of a cupful for an hour's pumping, it wouldn't keep us racing.

We had a spare pump for the water-maker. It was

installed on the main engine. The possibility was to try to transfer the pump over to the generator, and drive the water-maker off that. But it was a major engineering task, and would take a day or more to sort out. And even if we did get the pump installed, we would have the same problem getting the drive wheel tight. Worse, we just didn't have a day left to do the work. Everyone was being ground down by the dehydration. There was a simpler way, a quicker way, but we had no idea if it would work. We could transfer the hoses from the original pump to the pump driven by the main engine, and run the water-maker off that. It would take more diesel, but the water-maker only required an hour's running each day. We had enough fuel, so long as nothing else went wrong.

As we started work, I could see how much Lisa was suffering. Dehydration is an insidious disorder. It creeps up on you, and by the time you feel thirsty it's too late. The body is already working at well below its peak performance. Tiredness, a headache, nausea, giddiness all follow. Lisa was way past just feeling thirsty. And, combined with the responsibility, the stress of the situation fell very heavily on her shoulders. The physical strain of working in the heat and the tight spaces, with the boat constantly fighting her efforts, was dragging her down.

I tried to help her work through it slowly, taking our time over every step to make sure it was right. But nothing was as simple as it should have been. We had to attach the belts that drive the pump from the main engine, but they were the wrong length. We had to use the adjustable emergency spares, and they took two hours to stretch tight. The hoses would only

reach the pump through a hole that had to be cut in the floorboards. And all the time it was getting hotter. We took a couple of time-outs on deck, but fresh air does little to clear your head when it's simply drying out. We were becoming slower and slower, but just kept grinding away at it – and finally it was done.

We were totally exhausted now. We all knew that this was our last chance to keep racing. No one said it out loud – even while we struggled to switch the pump from the main engine to the generator – but if it didn't work we would have little choice but to turn back to the Cape Verde Islands. It would be too risky to carry on, but it would be an ignominious end to our first leg. Lisa turned the key and hit the starter to fire up the engine. The boat shook, the silence broken. On deck everyone froze. I couldn't count the times they had listened up there, hoping to hear a cheer of triumph. The pump rumbled into life and spluttered some water down the hose. It fed into the water-maker. A cough, a trickle, and fresh water flowed out the other end. Those first warm, slightly salty drops tasted like ice-cold spring water. And were twice as valuable.

The repair worked for the rest of the leg. It wasn't perfect: the spare pump couldn't manage the same pressure as the original; and the water had a slightly salty taste. But the girls went on to finish ninth, a day and a half ahead of Brunel Sunergy who had pulled into Recife, Brazil, to replace a rudder damaged in a collision with a whale. It wasn't the start they had hoped for, but there were eight more legs and a lot of miles still to race.

17

NEXT PAGE: THE 1997/98 WHITBREAD RACE STARTED IN SPECTACULAR FASHION,
WITH PERFECT CONDITIONS AND A HUGE
SPECTATOR FLEET THAT ESCORTED THE RACE BOATS OUT OF THE SOLENT.

ANNA DROUGGE NERVOUSLY AWAITS NEPTUNE'S GREETING AS SHE CROSSES THE EQUATOR FOR THE FIRST TIME. PERHAPS THE LAST TRADITIONAL CEREMONY STILL RESPECTED BY MODERN WHITBREAD SAILORS.

AS A WATCH CAPTAIN, LEAH NEWBOLD WAS ONE OF ONLY FOUR REGULAR HELMSMEN ON THE TWO WATCHES, EACH OF WHICH
CONSISTED OF FIVE PEOPLE WORKING A SIX-HOUR SHIFT DURING THE DAY, AND FOUR HOURS THROUGH THE NIGHT.

RELENTLESS ATTRITION OF EQUIPMENT MEANS ALMOST CONSTANT MAINTENANCE AND REPAIR WORK DURING THE TIME AT SEA:
BROKEN MAINSAIL BATTENS (ABOVE), TEMPORARY INSTALLATION OF WIND INSTRUMENTS (OPPOSITE).
PREVIOUS PAGE: IN THE HEAVY RUNNING CONDITIONS, ALL FIVE CREW ON DECK ARE FULLY OCCUPIED.
NEXT PAGE: AFTER THIRTY-FOUR DAYS AT SEA, THE CREW OF EF EDUCATION APPROACH CAPE TOWN.

THE SCHEDULE

33

October 11, five days after Lisa Charles's struggle with the water-maker. A tropical sun was pushing up over the horizon, announcing Day Twenty-one of the first leg of the 1997/98 Whitbread Race aboard EF Language. The men were barrelling along at a steady twelve knots with a reefed reaching headsail and a staysail. Two hundred and twenty-seven miles in front was the Isle da Trindade, the final point before the boats turn for Cape Town. EF Language had been reeling in the lead Merit Cup had on them for four days, and overnight they had stolen second place. Now they were three miles ahead and to leeward of Grant Dalton's crew. Only another three miles in front of EF Language was the leader for the last two weeks – Innovation Kvaerner. The fourth boat was Silk Cut – trailing a full 115 nautical miles behind after the leading three had made a breakaway move off Cape Finisterre two thousand miles previously.

Magnus:

'Hey, Magnus.' It was Curt's shout that brought me up the companionway. My watch had finished half an hour before, but I'd been a little slow about getting my head down in a bunk. Curt had the wheel, and when I looked back I could see that he wasn't happy about what was revealed by the orange glow of the morning sunshine. 'Why don't you get Rudi up here to take a look at this?' I glanced up at the puffy cumulus of a classic trade wind sky. But it was what lay in front that was the problem. The plain blue and white mix was replaced by a diffuse blend of clouds and colours: dark, arched, puff adders of clouds; white wisps of torn cotton with a flat grey, overcast backdrop; spectral light splintering off the towering cumulus lurching towards us. It was all bad news – clouds mess with the wind. I slid below and found Rudi. Paul was also awake, and he was ahead of us out of the hatch. We all stood staring at the ominous sky.

34

'Nothing on the fax charts or the digital weather files about this,' Rudi said in his considered Californian drawl.

'It may not be on the forecast, but it sure is here,' replied Paul. 'The breeze is coming ahead of us. Better start thinking about the light number one headsail.'

Josh was already moving, thrashing through the pile of sails on the windward side of the deck. He found the tail of the headsail bag and pulled. Juggy picked up the middle as the sail bag came clear and they trotted forward. In the time they took to find it, the sail change had gone from a possibility to an urgent necessity. The wind had shifted to the south, and the reaching headsail was forcing us off course. We were losing precious distance to the two boats lying to windward of us.

'Let's do it,' Cayard was urging everyone on.

I stepped into the pit to give them a hand, throwing off the halyard jammer holding up the staysail while Josh hauled the flapping cloth down to the deck. It was rolled and tossed below. Juggy plugged the new sail in and snapped the halyard on, while Josh ran the sheets aft. Kimo grabbed the rope from him, and dropped two turns on to the winch drum; Paul stepped automatically to the coffee-grinder handles that power it. Josh and I were already pulling the sail up. Hoisted, the new headsail was flapping lightly, the old one still pulling the boat forward at ten knots. I gave the halyard a final turn on the winch and wound it tight.

'Going with the reacher,' I yelled forward to Juggy, peeling the other halyard off the self-tailer. Juggy had the luff, Josh grabbed the leech. I snapped the cleat open and the old sail tumbled downwards. Frantic hands hauled it up and away from the guardrails and the snapping, foaming ocean below. The boat hesitated a little in her stride for a moment, before Paul whaled into the handles to wind the new sail tight and power the rig back up.

'That's good, guys,' said Curt from the wheel. 'Back on course.' But the work wasn't finished. The reaching headsail had to be packed, flaked into its bag. Everyone was breathing hard, sweat running into their eyes. The sun was barely showing itself over the horizon, but already it was cranking up the temperature. The first sail change was complete. It took ten minutes of flat-out work. We didn't know it then, but it was the first of eight we would complete in the next five hours. It was also the easiest.

As the boys on watch packed the sail and tidied the boat, I headed below, rather optimistically going for my bunk. But conditions were already changing, the wind was dropping and heading even further. I could feel the motion of the boat subtly change. A little more upright, a little less lively. Paul responded instantly. 'Magnus, dump the water, then we need to tack,' he yelled down the hatch.

The three tons of water that generate power by

'IT WAS ALL BAD NEWS – CLOUDS MESS WITH THE WIND.'

PAUL CAYARD WORKS WITH THE ON-DECK COMPUTER.

keeping the boat upright in a breeze were now just extra weight. It was slowing us down. I crawled to the switches, cranking the generator into life, smashing the quiet as it flushed the water out of the boat. 'Tacking,' I yelled to no one in particular. The off-watch stirred. There was shouting above, urgent voices, feet on the deck.

'Ready to tack, Magnus?' shouted Paul down the hatch.

'Clear to tack,' I called back as the last of the water gushed out. I snapped the valves shut and shook the shoulders of a couple of the off-watch who hadn't stirred. 'Swop sides,' I said. The boat sat upright and started to roll; there was a crash and clatter of winches. Now everyone below tore into the gear. Every single piece of movable weight had to be swopped to the new windward side to help keep the boat flat. And that included the sleeping crew. There was a quiet resignation; broken sleep was nothing new. The hull was full of movement. On deck the story was the same. All the sails had to be hauled across the boat and put in the stowage bags on the windward side. I could hear the effort that was going into the work on deck and matched it. Finally the boat reached its target speed once more, but the wind was relentless. It shifted again. We had to tack back.

There were four more tacks in the next forty minutes. At the moment, one followed another so fast that all the gear hadn't been shifted to the new side before we had to start shifting it back. There were no

tea-breaks on this watch. But finally the wind seemed to relent. It swung hard left, to the east, and increased. Now we could make the course easily. I could feel the boat pick up speed, and knew what was coming next. I stuck my head out of the hatch to see huge towering clouds all around, but I was looking for Paul. 'Spinnaker?' I asked.

'Three-quarter masthead,' he replied immediately.

Another sail change, and a difficult one. I brought the sail up on deck, and stayed to work the halyards again. I could see the strain on everyone's faces. Three hours now, without a break. The spinnaker was hoisted. For a few brief moments the boat settled down. But on it went. After this spinnaker was up the wind increased again and headed us. Now we changed to the Code A5, a masthead asymmetric. The first spinnaker joined the staysail and the headsail on the cabin floor. There was no time to pack either sail. The changes kept coming. The A5 came down. Now there were two spinnakers, a staysail and a headsail below. Still no time to pack anything. The wind became light; the water was drained out. It came back up and the water was pumped back in. The sequence was repeated again and again, along with endless subtle changes to the tanks to trim the boat. The clouds kept throwing it at us. And we all kept responding, dialling it up on the ballast tank valves, hurling the loose gear and cajoling the bodies around the boat.

Occasionally Rudi crawled through the carnage below to take a look on deck. He would compare what

35

below to take a look on deck. He would compare what he saw to the radar screen, suggest a course change that he hoped would keep us in the best breeze, and crawl back through the chaos. On deck Paul controlled everything from his station on the grinder. Decisions came fast and furiously, an instant response to every shift in the conditions. But there seemed no end to the shattered sky and the fickle demands of the wind. We got on the edge of a cloud and now we had a big breeze and the A6 had to be hoisted. It's a full-size masthead spinnaker, and it hauled us down the course.

No one expected it to last for long, and it didn't. A cloud moved towards us, the rain started and the wind dropped. But worse, much worse than before. The boat slowed and ground to a halt. The gennaker staysail went up as a windseeker. The lightest of sails – it gave the boat a couple of knots of speed. It was better than nothing. I pumped the tanks clear, and shifted the gear to leeward to try and heel the boat so gravity could give the sails some shape. But now it was 11.00, time to cook a meal. However bad it gets, the boat has to keep its routine. So I picked my way through thousands of yards of wet spinnaker cloth and found the food, pans and water.

Eventually the water was on the gas, and as I waited for it to boil I checked up on deck. The rain was teeming down, running in sheets off the mainsail, dripping in streams off the boom. I watched Juggy hesitate on his way to leeward to tip a puddle of water off the sail on to his face. Fresh water, a real luxury.

I stared into the rain and the gloom to windward. But it was impossible to see more than a hundred metres, never mind several miles. Merit Cup and Innovation Kvaerner were up there somewhere. Or were they? Did they have this cloud system? Or were they miles ahead, cruising smoothly along in steady trade winds? Josh muttered what we were all thinking, 'Man, I hope those other guys up there got this weather, or we're going to get our butts kicked.'

More work stopped us thinking about it. Three spinnakers and a headsail to pack. Josh and Juggy joined me below, everyone moving as gently as they could, trying not to disturb the delicate motion of the boat through the confused seas. My watch was starting to stir with an uneasy silence. Everyone knew we'd been through some bad weather. Everyone knew that the other boats might not have had it. The rain continued to pour down, plastering hair on to anxious, creased faces. While I was packing the spinnakers I forgot the cooking and carbonised the freeze-dried ingredients. The acrid smell of burnt food added itself to the steaming damp. But it was almost over. We crept out from under the glowering sky. The rain finally stopped. The clouds cleared, and the wind eased back into the south-east. There was one final sail change before the midday watch change, back to the reaching headsail and staysail that we started with six hours earlier.

I dropped down the ladder about half an hour after the watch change. The new off-watch were sitting in an exhausted silence. There was a click from on deck, as the reaching headsail was gently trimmed, but everyone's attention was directed aft, towards where Rudi awaited the midday position report. This was what it was all about. The schedule, or 'sched', a six-hourly report on the positions of the fleet, which included the distance gained or lost on the opposition. It makes each six-hour period a separate race – and the results come in on the satellite communications. For the people sailing the boat for that six-hour period, it's like receiving your exam results. And the tension was just as palpable. Everyone knew that the boat had been worked hard, and that good decisions had been made. But no one knew how local the cloud effect was. If the two boats to windward had sailed straight past it in clean wind, then it was all for nothing. No one could sleep; no one had tried. There was a noise aft. Rudi stuck his head out of the navigation station.

'Well?' demanded Josh, who was closest. But he already knew it was good news.

Rudi couldn't hide the smile, he's under strict instructions not even to try. 'We had a ten-mile lead at midday.'

'Yes!' someone shouted, punching a fist in the air.

There was a wash of visible, physical relief and pleasure. Everyone was smiling now. The news went up on deck.

'We're winning this race, don't you guys go losing it for us.'

And they didn't. Not on that watch, or the next. Merit Cup came back at them on the approach to the island, but Language rounded Trindade with a half-mile lead and fought for two days to get south, into the path of an oncoming low-pressure system. They picked up the breeze first and extended their lead, first five miles, then ten, twenty, thirty – the distance piled up as the scheds rolled in. EF Language was to win the first leg of the 1997/98 Whitbread Race by a full twenty hours. It was a good start.

Merit Cup followed them into Cape Town twenty hours later, then Innovation Kvaerner and Silk Cut. BrunelSunergy's whale damage was the most eventful thing on a quiet leg. But all that changed in Cape Town, where America's Challenge was forced to pull out of the race for financial reasons, and Chris Dickson was replaced as skipper of Toshiba by former watch captain Paul Standbridge. Nine boats would line up for Leg Two.

37

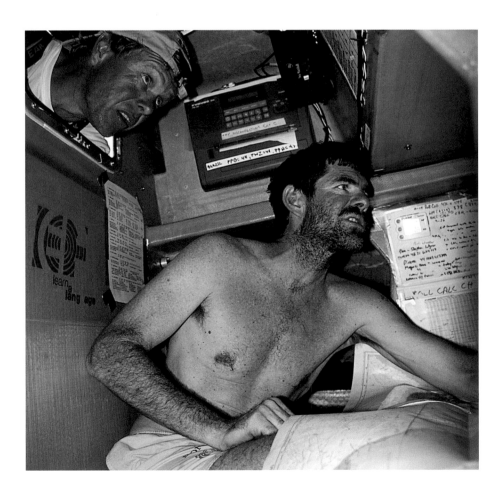

MAGNUS OLSSON CHECKS WITH MARK RUDIGER, TO SEE IF THE SCHEDULE HAS ARRIVED.

NEXT PAGE: EF LANGUAGE LEADS THE FLEET OUT OF THE SOLENT.

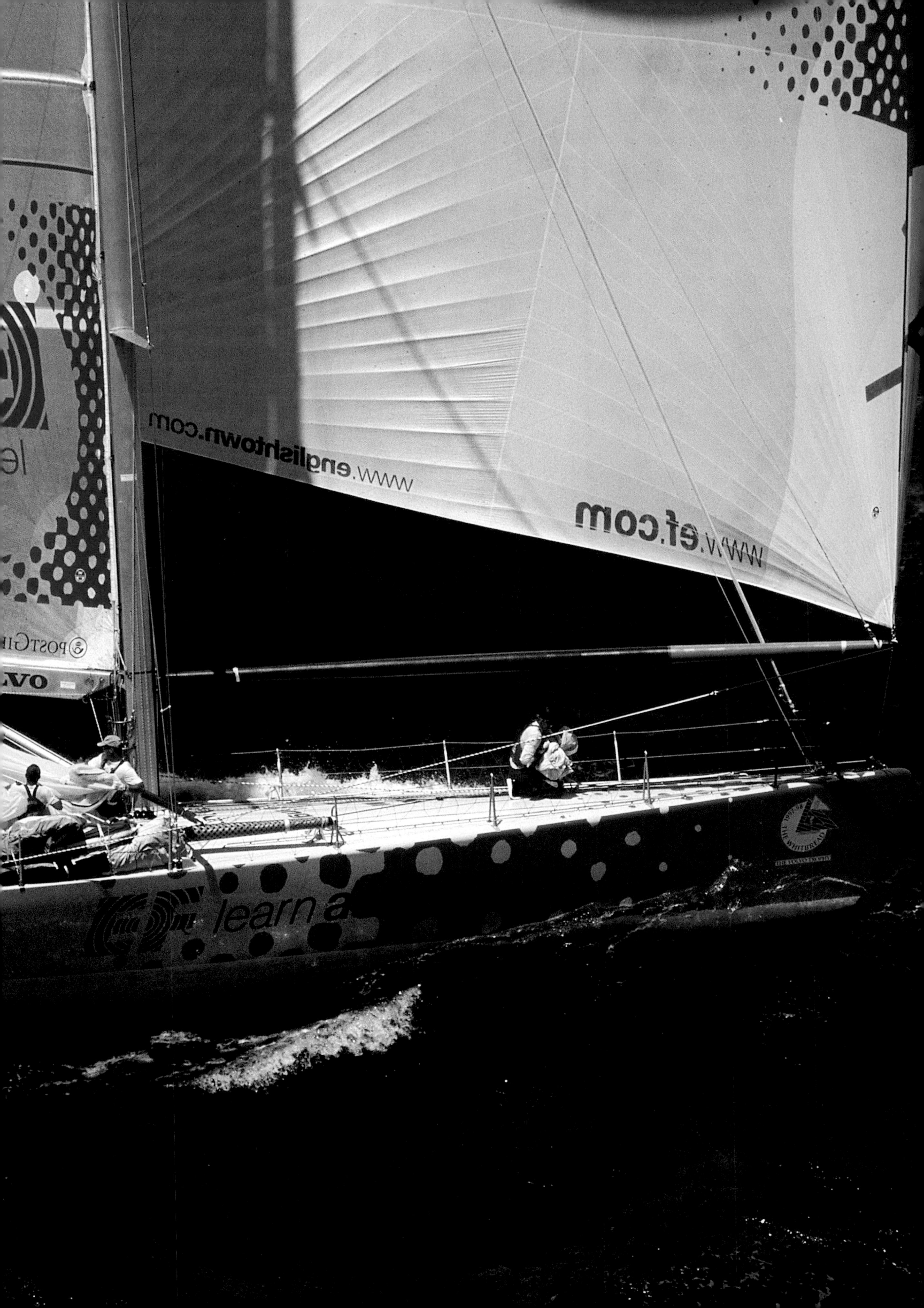
www.englishtown.com
www.ef.com
learn a

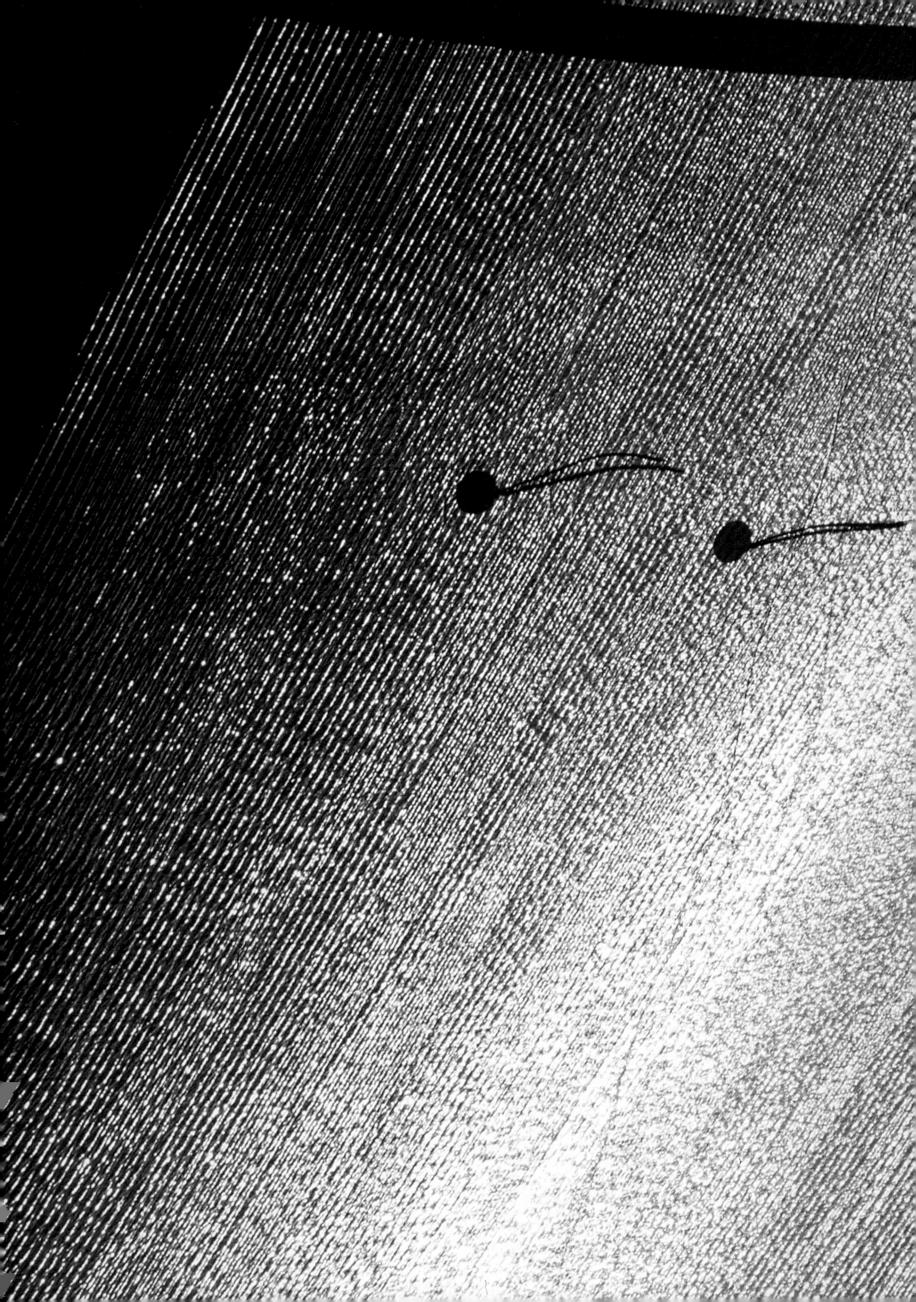

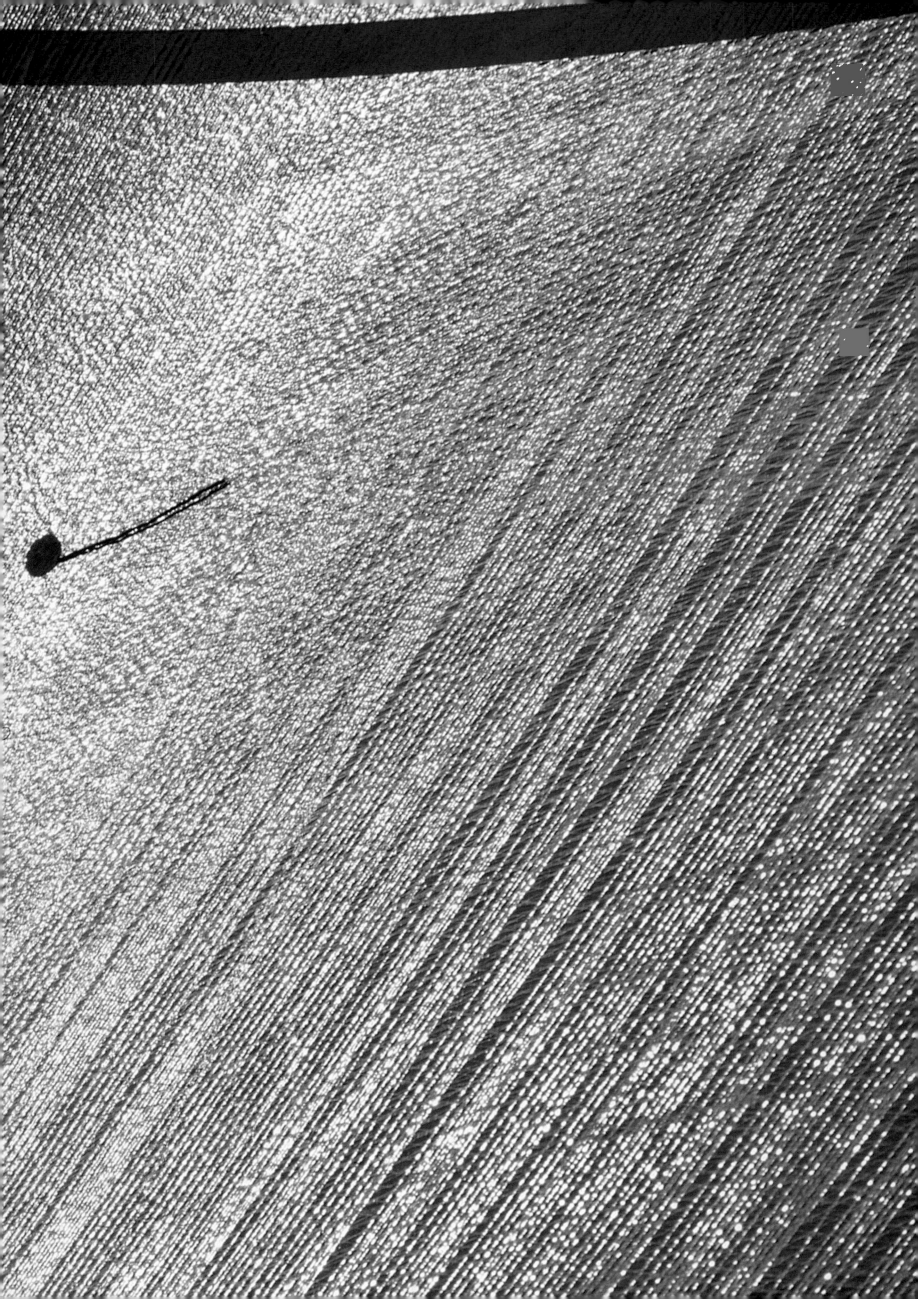

THIS UPWIND HEADSAIL CHANGE REQUIRED THE ENTIRE WATCH ON THE FOREDECK, WITH THE EXCEPTION OF THE HELMSMAN.

NEXT PAGE: EF LANGUAGE CELEBRATE THEIR FIRST LEG VICTORY IN CAPE TOWN.

STACK OVERBOARD

Day Thirteen, Leg Two, Cape Town to Fremantle through 4,600 nautical miles of the Southern Ocean. The warmth and vivid colours of the African continent were a hazy memory – everything was grey. The sky was overcast, a broken, patchwork grey. The water was a deep, chilling, relentless grey. Even the weak daylight seemed grey. With the wind-speed nudging the top end of the twenties, EF Education was cracking along under a full masthead spinnaker. But so far, it hadn't been windy enough. The low-pressure systems that normally fling the boats around the Antarctic had remained tantalisingly out of reach through the first half of the leg. Trapped in high pressure and light air trying to escape Cape Town, the girls had struggled to get south. The standings showed they were in last place, calculated as distance to the finish. But it's not always about who's closest to the finish, it's about who's set up for the weather. And when a cold front did finally break down the high pressure, Education was perfectly positioned to take advantage of it. They picked up the breeze and were now in the middle of the main pack, only thirteen miles behind Merit Cup, locked in a battle for seventh place as they rounded the south-eastern edge of the Kerguelen Islands.

Anna:

The boat was flying, lunging down the wave faces and shooting a huge rooster tail of spray into the air.

I'd been steering through the last couple of hours of the watch, with Emma trimming the kite. And after six hours on deck together, we'd really tuned into the conditions and each other. It required absolute concentration and a huge physical effort. So I heard rather than saw Christine stick her head through the aft hatch and call for a gybe. We were sailing north-east on port, but the wind had been slowly shifting round from the west to the south-west. I'd been steering the same downwind angle, and so following the wind shift meant a more northerly course. But we needed to hold south a little longer to position properly for the next low-pressure system – and that meant a gybe to starboard. Christine was picking her moment carefully: the coming watch change meant there would be extra people available without the need to get anyone

dressed specially. I shuddered involuntarily at the thought of them climbing out of warm sleeping bags and into freezing cold, wet clothes. It was the worst time.

Leah had repeated the order for those forward, and Lisa was already working on the spinnaker sheets while Leah began to haul the sails to leeward. There was nearly a ton of them on deck, all stacked and tied down to a row of pad-eyes on the outboard edge of the boat. They were moved so that they would be on the new windward side, as the boat came out of the gybe. Katie and Kiny emerged on deck and helped Leah; Christine and Lynneth quickly followed them. The final job was for everyone to take up their normal positions. Christine took the wheel from me, and I went on to the spinnaker sheet.

'OK, bring in the main,' yelled Christine, as she bore away to bring the boat almost square to the wind. I eased the spinnaker sheet into the turn to keep the sail full. Katie had stepped onto the mainsheet winch grinder to help Kiny bring the sail in. Conditions were marginal for gybing with the big 1.5 ounce masthead chute up, and there was no way it could be done without the mainsail being pulled into the centreline first. Otherwise, the wind would fling the sail across the deck so fast it would rip the mast out of the boat. But the time spent waiting for the mainsail to come in was the most dangerous. The boat was slow and vulnerable

because of the abnormal sail setting. So the two of them went as hard as they could on the handles, while we waited tensely for the moment. Pounding, sweating and grinding as they were, the mainsail seemed to come in so terribly slowly, a huge wing being hauled in against the weight of wind that was filling it.

But it was almost there, and Christine was looking for a good wave to spin the wheel on. Then I heard her shout as she felt the first bubble of trouble on the rudder. The stern of the boat was lifting under my feet – an awkward angle, heeled to leeward as the wave built under the windward quarter. The heel forced the boat to try to turn to windward, and that exposed more of the main to the wind and heeled us further. It was a vicious circle that could quickly lead to a broach. Christine reacted instantly. 'Ease main!' she yelled, spinning the wheel hard to try to stop the turn as the heel steepened. Kiny dived for the self-tailer that held the rope in the top of the winch.

I desperately paid out the spinnaker sheet as the boat leant harder into the turn, the rope searing through my fingers. The drum whined as the sheet eased, the groan echoing round the boat. The huge spinnaker shook itself once, then momentarily filled as a blast of air popped round the mainsail. The snap load from the spinnaker loosened the final tenuous grip the rudder had on the water – and Christine had on control. There

AT SPEED, DEEP IN THE SOUTHERN OCEAN, THE SATCOM C PROVIDED A RELIABLE LINK WITH THE OUTSIDE WORLD.

'TRAPPED IN HIGH-PRESSURE AND LIGHT AIR TRYING TO ESCAPE CAPE TOWN ...' THE SPECIALIST MASTHEAD REACHING SPINNAKERS KEPT THE BOAT POWERED UP IN LIGHT AIR, BUT WERE VERY DIFFICULT TO HANDLE.

was nothing more that would save us. We spun out and crashed.

I knew the signs and was already grabbing for the guard-rail as the deck slid away underneath me, turning into a steep, vertical wall. The leeward rail was digging deep into the grey Southern Ocean, water foaming down the sidedeck towards the stacked sails in a solid wall. I saw it reach the pile and keep going. Starting from the front, the wave simply peeled them off the deck and flung them over the side of the hull – popping the stanchions out of the way like matchwood.

The boat staggered like a wounded animal as she slowed and stopped, the huge mass of sails acting like a giant handbrake in the water. Christine regained some control and held the boat feathered into the wind. But the masthead spinnaker was shaking us like a dog with a rag doll. It was slowly pulling the boat forward. And with two-thirds of the sail inventory hanging off a few lengths of sail-tie and the pad-eyes that attached them to the deck, even that slow movement was enough to increase the strain to breaking point. The spinnaker had to come down before something gave way – the mast, sail-ties or the spinnaker itself.

Up at the bow, Lisa and Marleen told me later that they hadn't even noticed the sails were in the water – their concern was solely focused on the spinnaker. I lurched down the steeply angled deck to help them, while Lisa led the second sheet round the bow as a spinnaker take-down line. I took it from her, as Marleen was struggling to clear the halyard, ready to drop the sail. But the spinnaker had other plans. Just when Lisa got to the bow to fire the sail away, the halyard gave up the unequal struggle to stay in one piece. The bang of its failure was all the louder for the sudden silence that

followed as the unleashed spinnaker floated gently, almost regally, into the ocean to leeward. If it had been serious before, now it was teetering on a catastrophe.

Help was at hand. Three of the off-watch, half-dressed, joined us to try to pull the huge, sodden sail out of the water. The loose sheet was used to winch the spinnaker closer. But once it was in our hands, thousands of square feet of sailcloth had to be manually hauled back into the boat. With the waterproof gloves it was almost impossible to get a decent grip on the sail. For every couple of feet we pulled in, one slipped back into the ocean. Even with six of us, it seemed to take for ever. We were sweating profusely in the fearsome cold. And while all this was going on forward, the rest of the crew were establishing the fact that there was no way six, or even all twelve of us, could lift a ton of sodden sails back into the boat unaided.

But we were winning our grim fight at the bow, and slowly the situation went from dramatic and desperate to just desperate. With the spinnaker safely below, the boat slowed and almost stopped. She was sitting, nearly head to wind, with the mainsail luffing and the mast safe. That relieved the pressure on the sail-ties, and with the extra ropes the other girls had got on the bag handles it no longer looked like we would lose the lot. That was the good news. The bad news was that, battered by the waves and stationary in the Southern Ocean, every minute we were stuck there Merit Cup was putting yards on us. But however much we hated it, there was no getting round the fact that we were limited by our physical strength. We couldn't just heave the sails back on board. The problem was going to take some sorting out. And doing so meant working close to the edge of the boat with no guard-rails, so those who had rushed on deck without

FOUL-WEATHER GEAR IS EASY TO PUT ON AND WARM, UNLESS YOU'RE IN THE WATER (LEFT). FORTUNATELY LEAH NEWBOLD
(RIGHT) WAS WEARING HER SURVIVAL SUIT WHEN SHE WENT OVERBOARD TO HELP RECOVER THE SAIL STACK.

harnesses or oilskins were sent back below to gear up.

The only help that was available in the middle of this Southern Ocean wasteland was the winch gear. Somehow we had to fasten halyards and sheets round the whole package and wind it up and out of the water. Leaning over the side, with someone holding on to your ankles, it was possible to slide a halyard between the boat and the sails. But it was quickly clear that someone would have to get into the water to find the other end. Leah already had her boots off. Dressed in a survival suit – with sealed feet, wrists and neck – we attached a sheet round her waist so we could pull her back on board if she became detached from the boat. She added a huge lifejacket, almost disappearing under all the clothes and equipment.

Then she slipped into the icy water, gasping with the cold even through the survival suit. I watched her plunge straight under the grey sea, not sure whether it was worse on deck (anxiously awaiting her reappearance), or in the water, fumbling in the darkness for the rope end, breath held, heart pounding, sail bags and boat lurching about above you, threatening to trap you, crush you. But that was the worse moment of the clear-up. It's the things that happen quickly, like the original broach, that are the most frightening. Sorting out the mess is mostly just hard work.

Nevertheless, it was a massive relief for everyone when she reappeared, spluttering, coughing and cursing. Then the halyard twitched on the deck and snaked out over the edge of the boat as she dragged it through and waved it above her head.

'All right, go Leah.' someone muttered.

I think it was Lisa who grabbed the halyard end from her. It was quickly pulled through and fastened on itself. Other willing hands hauled Leah out of the water. More ropes were attached to the soaked bundle, sheets criss-crossed the boat to winches and pulleys. The spinnaker foreguy system was pressed into service to pull the sails forward as they came clear.

The atmosphere was amazing, everyone was working together at once, fastening, tightening, tying, pulling and winding. There was no shouting, very little spoken instruction, just an urgent need in everybody's mind to get going again as fast as possible. And inch by inch the sails came clear until, with a final lurch and the roll of a wave, they landed on the deck. The boat popped upright and we had regained control. With the sails secured, a storm jib was hoisted to push the bow of the boat round on to the starboard tack. And once we were going the right way, the masthead spinnaker went straight back up. It had taken an hour and a half of total effort by all twelve crew to get moving again. The clearing up and repairing took longer, juggling stanchions to jury rig a guard-rail, and sorting through the sails. But that didn't matter, what mattered was that we were moving fast, and in the right direction.

In the next schedule they had lost eighteen miles to Merit Cup. And in the end the physical power and experience of the Merit Cup crew pulled them ahead in the hard running conditions of the Southern Ocean. But Grant Dalton knew they'd had a fight on their hands, and acknowledged his respect for the crew of Education at the finish-line press conference. And the women were happy with the eighth place – they'd been in the thick of it on a tough Southern Ocean leg, and they were improving fast.

53

NEXT PAGE: REEFING THE MAINSAIL NEEDED EVERY WINCH AND THE EXTRA HANDS OF NAVIGATOR LYNNATH BECKLEY, TAILING FOR KERYN MCMASTER.

UPW!ND AND DOWNWIND, REGULAR CHECKS FOR CHAFING AND FATIGUE CAN SAVE SERIOUS FAILURES AND DOWNTIME.

IN THE WORST CONDITIONS, SURVIVAL SUITS AND SAFETY HARNESSES WERE MANDATORY ON DECK.

NEXT PAGE: SEEING THE OMINOUS CLOUD ON THE HORIZON, BRIDGET SUCKLING ANTICIPATES AND PREPARES FOR A SAIL CHANGE.

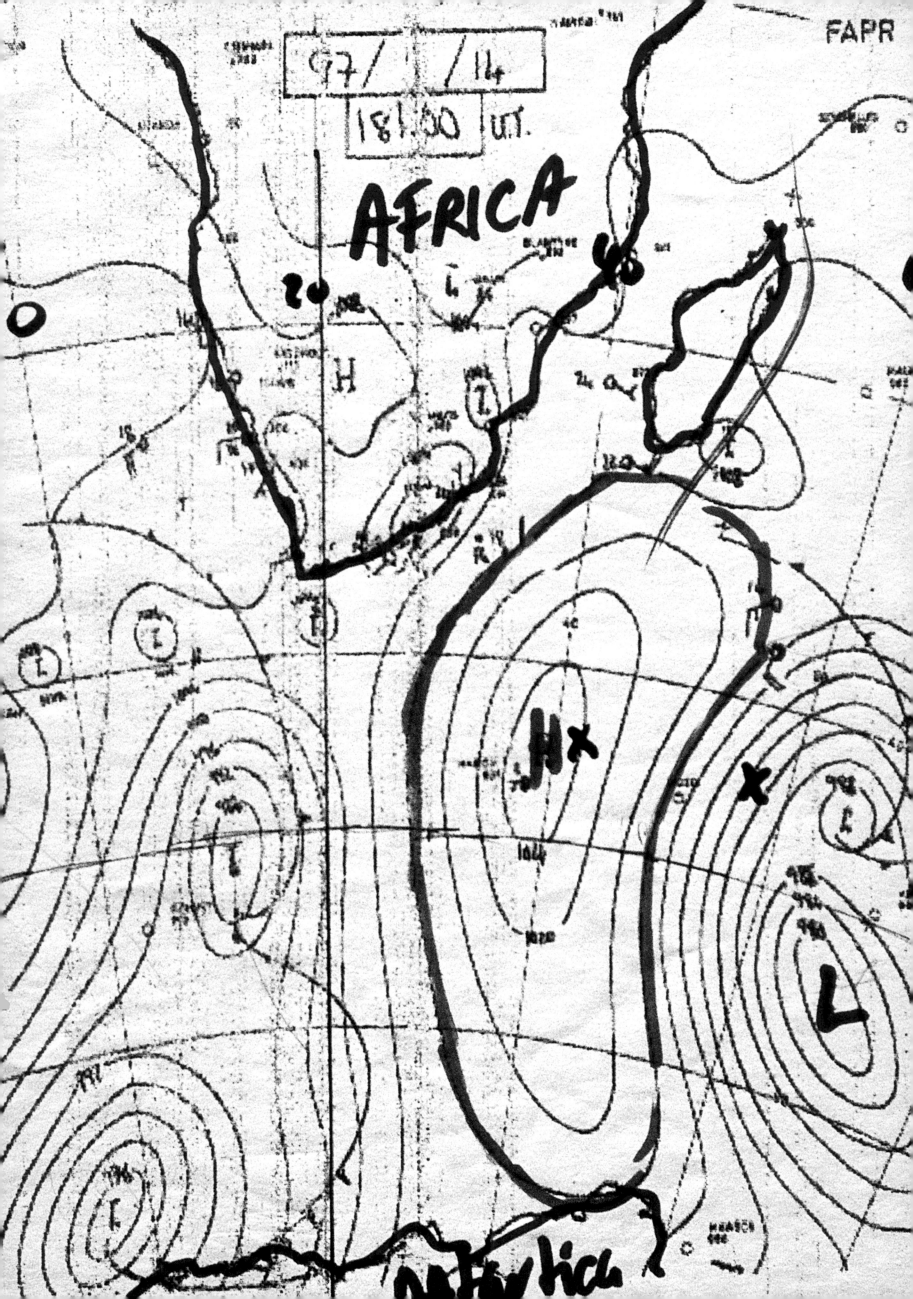

OVER THE LINE

EF Language had also been trapped by the high pressure at Cape Town. But only after she had let the opportunity to escape slip through her fingers on the second night, when the crew had sailed east rather than south. Languishing in eighth, they had watched Swedish Match, Innovation Kvaerner and Toshiba establish apparently unassailable leads for the first three places. But then Cayard and Rudiger had staged a brilliant strategic recovery during the following week to get back to fourth place. Now they were defending that fourth against a charging Silk Cut. With Innovation Kvaerner looking a certain second, EF Language needed fourth to maintain her overall lead. And the team aboard EF Language also found themselves tested to their limits by the Southern Ocean.

Magnus:

The previous two nights
had been bad enough. During the first of those, conditions had been so extreme that we had only been able to set a blast-reaching headsail with a full mainsail and staysail. During one furious moment, a wave had swept down the boat and torn me away from the wheel. I was thrown against the aft guard-rails, at the full extent of the lifeline. With everyone else facing forward and also struggling to recover from the wave, no one had noticed that the boat was careering through the Southern Ocean on her own. If the balance of the sail trim forced her to bear away it would be a total disaster. Howling into a gybe at full speed, the main would sweep across the deck, taking out the backstay, the mainsail battens, the mast and anyone standing in the way. But there was no time to think about any of that. I just knew I had to get back to the wheel. I struggled, like a punch-drunk fighter, off the guard-rails and back to the helm. But as soon as I got there I knew it was all right, just from the touch. The wheel was motionless, rudder on the centreline, the boat was perfectly balanced

– smoking through the Southern Ocean straight as an arrow. It was a close-run thing, but the following night we were not so fortunate. We broached twice and with thirty-five to forty knot winds sweeping the decks, both of them were violent affairs. The first wipe-out had trashed the A5 – a masthead spinnaker. The second did for the A9, along with the spinnaker pole. The problem was not just the downtime spent with the boat on its side, the real cost was the eighteen hours it took to repair the damage. The broken sails were taken control of down below, with Marco trying to find the pieces to put them back together. Paul had to stand his watch on deck, doubling his workload. The routine of the boat was badly disrupted, with the sail everywhere – it couldn't even be trodden on. Simple necessities like hot drinks became a luxury as we all tried to avoid disrupting the repair work.

But we came through a desperate forty-eight hours with most of the lead intact. Silk Cut was still forty miles behind, and eventually the normal routine was re-established, with everything repaired. The wind had eased slightly, although the squalls were still vicious. With the A8 storm spinnaker set we were operating with the smallest margins of safety, pushing the very limits of the boat's capacity for speed, launching her through a black, black night, filled with icy spray, a vicious freezing wind and waves the size of houses.

I was guiding her through this extreme environ-ment, barricaded behind oilskins, survival suit and ski-mask, led only by the faint red glow of the digital instrument read-outs and the deepest rooted instincts. Surging to the top of a wave, the rig would emerge from the troughs of the ocean swell; mainsail and spin-naker would feel the blast just as the boat slowed at the top of its climb. This was always a critical moment. The boat was at her most unstable when she was going slowly with the sails heavily loaded. The trimmers had to see this coming, and ease the sheets to keep the boat upright as the wind pounced. The slightest hesitation and I would find the highly pressured sails transfer-ring the load straight into the rudder – then it was a brutal fight to keep her going straight. And once we topped the crest and started to lurch down the face I needed every ounce of control I could get. The boat would accelerate like a sixty-foot, fifteen-ton surfboard falling into the pit of a thirty-foot drop.

Each time the boat plunged down I was faced with an instant decision. And for each decision the trim-mers and grinders had to know what it was, almost before I made it. If I went straight they had to be ready to ease the sails. Failure would mean a nose-dive and tons of water sweeping across the deck – slowing the boat as though we had sailed into a giant honey pot. If I bore away they had to sheet the main tighter. Otherwise the boat could turn too far and spin into a vicious and potentially lethal gybe. If I luf-

EXTREME CONDITIONS MAKE IT IMPOSSIBLE EVEN TO STAND UP.

MARCO CONSTANT PREPARES THE SEWING MACHINE FOR ONE IN A MARATHON SEQUENCE OF SAIL REPAIRS.

fed up they had to ease the sails instantly to stop the boat simply blowing over and wiping out. In these conditions – so close to the edge, so much of the time – a hesitation lasting only fractions of a second would mean disaster. But on this watch there were no hesitations. There was only perfect anticipation by the trimmers. Perfect understanding of each and every move by all of us. And the boat was loving it.

I thought the bad days were over. I was sure that we were matching Silk Cut wave for wave, yard for yard. It was a fantastic feeling – we were back in control of the Southern Ocean. I went below at the end of the watch, stripped off the top couple of layers of clothing down to the mid-layer fleece, and crawled into my sleeping bag exhausted. All around me the boat still resounded to the battle that was going on above. The hull reverberated to the water flushing past it at over twenty knots. I lay and stared at the ceiling in the darkness, listening to the winches grind and churn, to the schung, schung noise as the sheet was eased off the drum, the whole boat shaking to the sudden release of power and pressure. I felt the lurch and wobble of the hull as it responded, then heard a crash and roar as the boat took off down the wave face, juddering from the acceleration. It was almost impossible to sleep as the cacophony rang through the hull.

But soon there was a subtle change in the noise. The tempo increased slightly, then quickly. I could hear the voices on deck.

'Big pressure on you,' yelled hoarsely.

Then more urgently, 'Big gust!' A curse. 'Thirty-eight knots, still building. Big pressure, look at the goddam speed! You wanna blow it!'

'No, I've got it! I've got it. Ease! Ease!'

The winch drum howled. The boat had shaken herself at a frequency that shouldn't have been physically possible for something that size, and then taken off. The note of the whole boat changed, the pitch of the vibration clattering pencils and dividers out of the navigation station, rattling teeth and gums. I grabbed the edge of the bunk, tensing my legs against the bulkhead. I could feel the others doing the same. If we lost it at this speed it would be really messy. But somehow I knew they wouldn't.

'Forty knots, wind speed still building.' The voice was calmer now, almost surreally calm.

'Stay on the vang.'

'Forty-two knots!' A note of alarm again.

'I've got her.'

'Don't see more pressure. Steady at this, forty-three knots.'

Then we hit the back of the wave with a surge of deceleration. Tons of water threw itself aft down the deck and I felt my knees load up as I was pushed into the bulkhead. The winches whined again as the sheets were dumped. But she stayed level and fast, flinging the water off and pounding over the crest. My stomach was in my mouth and my back lifting off the bunk as the boat dropped, airborne, into the next trough. The rollercoaster ride from hell.

It went on like that for another five minutes as the squall blew through, with everyone below holding their breath. When the windspeed finally subsided to a more normal thirty-five knots, the change seemed like silence – and I was instantly asleep, happy that the boys had it all under control. And just as surely I knew everything had changed the moment I woke up. It was tangible – in the air, in the voices, in the hand on my shoulder. The speed of the boat was down but the windspeed was still up. Language was stumbling under the weight of the wind without enough sail power to be able to accelerate to her natural speed. The voice in my ear was loud and urgent. 'We broke the A8, not badly, it just tore when it refilled after collapsing. We took it down. Paul wants to go with the A7 ...' A hesitation. 'I'm not so sure ...'

But it was Paul's decision. I shook myself fully awake, forced to return to a frantic world of sensory overload. I fumbled and dredged through the red shadowy light and the broken A8 spinnaker to gather my foul-weather gear. Around me others were doing the same. There were mutterings as the A7, a slightly larger fractional spinnaker, was called up on deck.

'Pretty damn windy for the A7,' someone said.

Then Paul's voice cut through the gloom. 'Got to do it. If we pole out the blast-reacher Silk Cut will be right on us by the time we get this fixed.'

The alternative to using the spinnaker was to put the small reaching headsail back up, and use the spinnaker pole to force it out to windward, where the spinnaker would normally fly. But we knew it was at least two knots slower than the spinnaker. For each of the six or seven hours it would take to repair the broken sail, the two or three miles we would give away would be enough to allow Silk Cut to catch right up with us. So with Silk Cut bearing down in his imagination, fully powered up and flying, Paul was pushing hard to get the spinnaker hoisted, but it was still a reluctant and anxious new watch that joined the men already on deck, as all hands prepared for the set. The magical mood of earlier was broken. And in the Southern Ocean, if you don't believe – in yourself, in your crew-mates – if you hesitate, you've already lost.

Curtis Blewitt was up the mast taping up the head-foil when the spinnaker was ready to hoist. Someone screamed into the black night to ask him if he would stay up there to 'strop off' the sail – that is, fasten a rope strop to the head of the spinnaker to take the load off the halyard. But as the sail was hoisted, the protective sock of cloth that stops it from opening and filling too early got caught on the guard-rail. It opened early. No one was ready. The snap of power from the spinnaker wiped the boat into a broach before the helmsman even had a chance to respond. The pole was loose because it was being moved aft, and it was instantly pulled upwards, breaking the end fitting.

But that was only the start. We lay on our side with a 2.2 ounce spinnaker that refused to break and refused to come down, being shaken like a wildebeest in the jaws of a crocodile. It's impossible for me to

71

describe or even imagine what it was like for Curtis lashed to the mast sixty feet off the deck, every bone being slowly shaken from its joints or smashed into the mast or rigging.

Someone was screaming, 'Cut the halyard.' And in the darkness the halyard was cut. The flogging spinnaker should have quieted as it tore itself free and blew away downwind. It didn't, it was the wrong halyard. I think we all thought, in that sickening moment, that Curtis was going to die. He was now sliding down the mast in an accelerating fall that would peel open his bear-like grip on the spar and throw him into the ocean. It was Rudi that saw the third halyard snaking off a winch. Curtis had also clipped the spare to his harness to bring it back down to the deck. Rudi lunged, and forty feet above him the fall was brought up short.

We got Curtis down in one piece on the spare halyard, but only after the spinnaker tore itself apart in the Southern Ocean gale. He had been lucky, we'd all been lucky. And we had to acknowledge that this time the Southern Ocean had beaten us. Paul felt he had pushed too hard. Perhaps he had. But if you don't, you won't win, because someone else surely will. And it is such a fine line between pushing hard and pushing too hard. If the A8 hadn't got that little tear, there would have been no decision to make about the A7. With no hoist, there would have been no broach, no broken sail

and gear to mend, no terrifying ordeal for Curtis, no man in a bunk suffering from shock and bruises. And Silk Cut would never have passed us. We all learnt some hard lessons in that hoist. Whether or not we had learnt them well enough, we would only find out on Leg Five, when we went back into the Southern Ocean.

During this desperate experience, Silk Cut was on her way to setting a record for the twenty-four hour distance run by a monohull: 449.1 nautical miles. She went past Language later that day. By the time Cayard's shaken and exhausted crew had fixed all the broken gear, Silk Cut was out of reach in what turned out to be a straight forward sail to the finish. The leg winner was Swedish Match, who had snatched the lead right off the start line in Cape Town, and held it to the finish. Swedish Match also posted the highest average speed for any Whitbread leg in twenty-five years: thirteen knots. Innovation Kvaerner and Toshiba's move south straight after Cape Town established them in second and third places. Language held the fifth place that Silk Cut pushed her back into, and she was followed in by Chessie Racing and then Merit Cup, just ahead of EF Education and BrunelSunergy. But it was a battered fleet that limped into Fremantle. Silk Cut and Language had lost stanchions when the sail stack had torn loose. Swedish Match, Innovation Kvaerner and Chessie Racing all hit whales.

73

CURTIS BLEWETT IS HOISTED ALOFT TO TRY AND HELP UNFOUL THE BADLY TWISTED SPINNAKER,

WRAPPED AROUND THE FORESTAY (OPPOSITE).

NEXT PAGE: RUNNING DOWNWIND AT HIGH SPEED IN HEAVY WEATHER, STACKING THE SAILS TO WINDWARD INCREASES

THE STABILITY, BUT DOESN'T HELP PREVENT THE BOW PLOUGHING INTO WAVES.

FREMANTLE

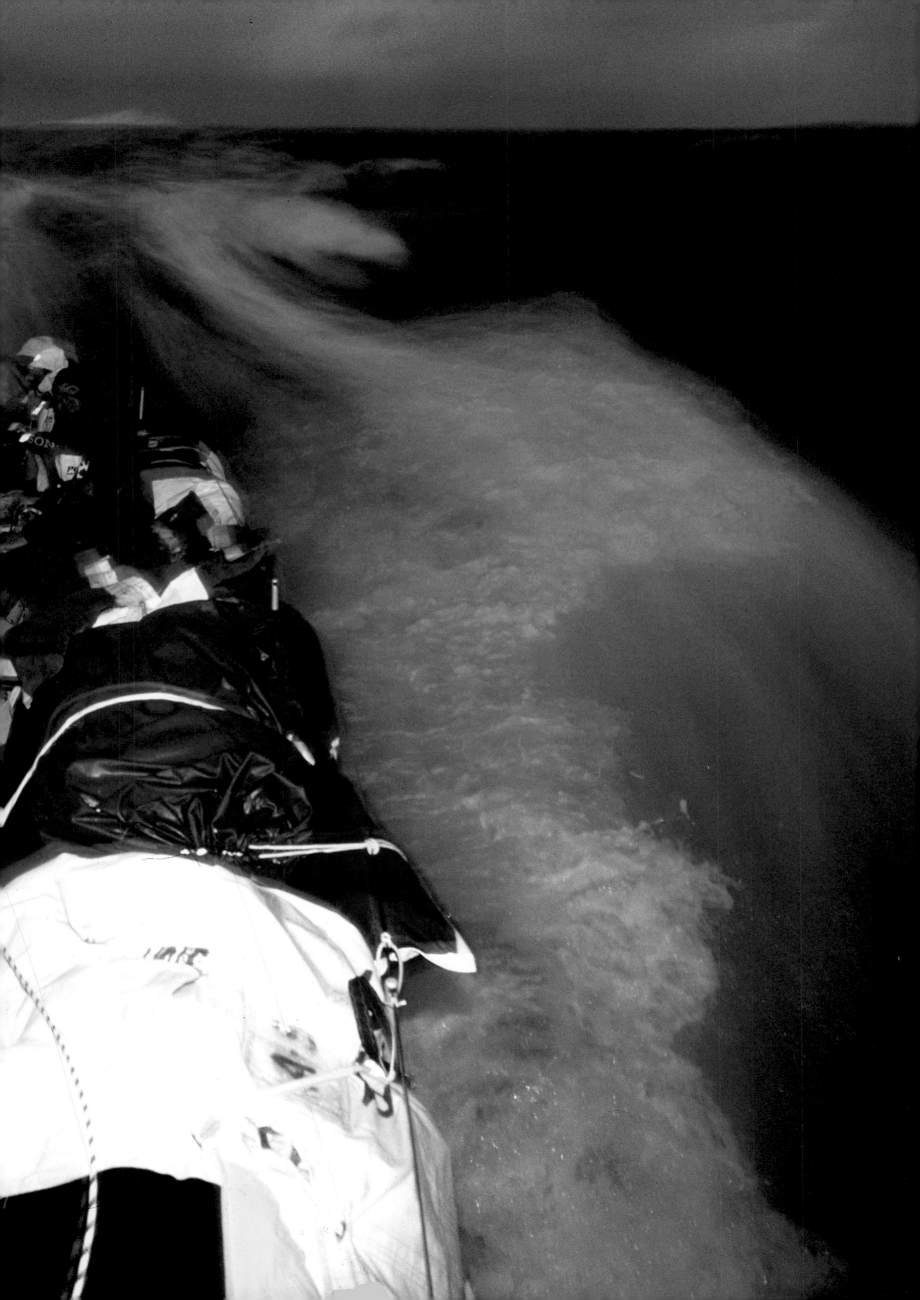

PREVIOUS PAGE: ON THE LIMIT OF CONTROL, COMPLETE COORDINATION BETWEEN THE TRIMMERS
AND THE HELMSMAN IS ESSENTIAL TO PREVENT A DANGEROUS WIPE-OUT.
BLINDED BY SPRAY, THE HELMSMAN MUST RELY ON HIS OTHER SENSES TO STEER THE BOAT FAST (OPPOSITE).
THE DAMAGE TO THE WHEEL WAS SUSTAINED WHEN A CREWMAN WAS WASHED DOWN THE
DECK AND SLAMMED INTO THE STEERING PEDESTAL (ABOVE).

PREVIOUS PAGE: BOWMAN CURTIS BLEWETT FIGHTS TO RETRIEVE THE SPINNAKER SOCK.
BATTERED BY WAVES IN FREEZING CONDITIONS FOR DAYS ON END, SOUTHERN OCEAN SAILING IS
ALL ABOUT STAMINA (ABOVE AND RIGHT).

NEXT PAGE: THE AMOUNT OF CLOTHING REQUIRED TO STAY WARM CAN MAKE THE SIMPLEST SAIL HANDLING A DESPERATE BATTLE – WHICH ONLY TEAM WORK CAN WIN.

SETTING UP A SECOND SHEET LEAD ON THE RAIL FOR PERFECT SAIL TRIM.

SLIM MARGINS

Leg Three: the first and longest of the 'sprint' legs, 2,250 nautical miles from Fremantle to Sydney in Australia. EF Language won the second of three starts and held the early lead as she left the coast of Western Australia. Others took up the running for periods in the Great Australian Bight, as the fleet spread itself across two hundred miles in a north/south line. But as the fleet converged onto Bass Strait, closing on Wilson's Promontory, EF Language was once again in front. Remarkably this convergence found no more than forty miles between the front and rear of the fleet. With seven boats tucked safely in behind EF Language, the danger came from Swedish Match, which was closing in on them from a position to the south. As Day Eight drew to a close, the wind dropped and conditions became more difficult. EF Language stopped completely overnight and as the sun began its climb over the horizon the atmosphere on board was anxious.

Magnus:

The first indication was on the radar. Rudi picked up a target five miles ahead. There was no telling what or who it was, but he had a bad feeling about it that he couldn't help transmitting to the rest of the crew. The unknown blip was comfortably pacing us, same speed, same course – never a good sign. We were six on deck as the sky slowly brightened, and I swept the horizon with binoculars. Paul had changed to the 'inshore' watch system the previous day. Curt dropped out to 'float' – on call at any time along with Paul and Rudi. The rest of us formed three watches of three people, with two watches up at once: an inshore variation on the Swedish system. That gave us a minimum of six people on deck rather than five, with the potential for nine when they were needed, rather than just seven. It cut down heavily on sleep, and couldn't be sustained through a long-distance race. But with every place from first to last to be taken or lost, we had decided to throw everything at it.

We didn't realise then that the race was going to get even tighter. I found the blip through the glasses. There's something very unmistakable about Whitbread 60s: the Kevlar sails, the huge roach … There was no doubt that it was Swedish Match. Turning, I scanned the horizon aft, and picked up one, two, three boats. I lowered the binoculars, a churning feeling in the pit of my stomach. It didn't take the schedule to confirm what we all knew in our hearts. The fleet had compressed massively overnight, and not only had we lost the lead, but the chasing boats were all within ten miles of us. It was going to be a glorious day's racing – or a desperate one.

The playing field was clearly defined. The coast of New South Wales lay in a north/south line to our west, with Sydney almost due north. Two major headlands projected out to the east, and between them lay long shallow bays. There was a southerly current against us offshore, while the wind was forecast to strengthen from the south, and then shift into the south-east as the thermal effect of the sun dragged it around. Initially, Paul played the offshore side of the course, and we consistently took a little distance, gybing downwind in the southerly breeze that was building up. Swedish Match's lead was pegged back by a mile and a half. Then we got a little greedy and pushed out once too far and too often. The wind shifted quickly to the south-east and we were caught off-

shore. Swedish Match pulled back about half of our gains as we were forced to sail extra distance – we were four miles behind.

It was a drag race to Point Perpendicular, the first headland that barred the route to Sydney. We were power reaching; it was all about stability – keeping the boat upright and flat, driving it as hard as possible. We dropped the watch system completely, and put everyone on deck, on to the 'rail' – the edge of the boat where their weight helped to keep the boat flat. Every piece of movable and legally stackable equipment was piled on to the windward side. The sails were all tied down on the windward deck. And finally, as the wind increased and the angle narrowed, the big masthead A6 spinnaker was hoisted to replace the lighter 0.5 ounce sail. The guys were full hiking; on the rail, legs and bodies extended through the lifelines to put every ounce of weight into increasing speed. Only one person was allowed off the rail at a time. If more than one was required below, to change trim or ballast, then Rudi was brought on deck to compensate.

Otherwise, Rudi was the only man down below. The questions peppered to him through the aft hatch were constant and demanding. The radar provided feedback on the gains and losses to both Swedish Match ahead and the chasing pack behind. It was these boats that would provide the earliest indication of where gains could be made, as they spread out

PAUL CAYARD AND MARK RUDIGER DISCUSS TACTICS AND STRATEGY WITH THE HELP OF THE ON-DECK COMPUTER.

behind us, looking for the edge that would get them back into contact. Would there be a better breeze offshore? Or would less adverse current inshore be more important? Rudi had constantly to track and plot everyone. He'd already been up for the best part of two days as we had negotiated difficult hurdles through the Bass Strait. And this was on top of a heavy head cold. But the commitment was paying off. The radar showed slow gains on both Swedish Match and the group behind.

Paul took the power that the big spinnaker provided and ran down with it to get to leeward of the boat ahead. With the wind steadily building towards twenty knots, we were creaming along – faster than Swedish Match, but sailing a more offwind course that was taking us closer to the coast. Neither of us were holding the line to Point Perpendicular, about twenty miles ahead. We weren't even trying, trading more speed for a lower course. In contrast, Swedish Match was giving up speed to try and hold on to a track around the headland. That strategy let us close the gap to less than a mile, although we were off to leeward of her. But as the wind continued to strengthen and shift into the south-east, it made it even more difficult to hold the course. Finally, it was clear that neither of us would lay the Point.

Both boats needed a smaller spinnaker – less sail area would allow us to sail closer to the wind, and get back on course. It was a crucial call. The right spinnaker could get us the lead back. The wrong one could lose it irrevocably. Too small a sail and we would be slow; too big and we would still be unable to make our course. Both mistakes would mean a second change, and because we were reaching, changing meant running off to leeward and a big loss of distance. This was where all the work before the start of

the race came in. The long hours of sail testing would truly pay off if we made the right call here.

The discussion went back and forth as the wind edged up and shifted. It could be the flatter masthead full-size spinnaker – the A5.5. Or maybe the smaller masthead spinnaker – the A5.3? Then there were two fractional sails, the A7 with a powerful downwind shape, and finally the A9, smaller than the A7 and a full two-thirds less sail area than the A6 - which we had up now. With the wind already pushing over twenty knots the A9 was the right sail in the gusts, but it was too small in the lighter stuff. Would the wind come up any more? Rudi was dragged into the discussion: more questions, more coolly considered answers. Pressure was building on a decision, we were flying up on Point Perpendicular. Paul committed us to the A9. With everybody totally focused on the chase, the sail change was a dream and we lost almost nothing.

But as soon as the new sail was up, Paul was unhappy. The boat felt under-powered – the sail was too small. We could see the boat-speed drop on the dial, and the radar blip of Swedish Match started to draw away. His frustration came through in his steering and the speed got worse. It was a downward spiral. Everyone urged patience and calm. We had to let the sail settle into the conditions, to find the new angle and motion through the waves, to let the speed build slowly, a little more with each surf. We couldn't give up on it straightaway, that would just be admitting defeat, accepting second place.

And slowly our situation improved. The speed built up until it matched that of the old sail, but the course was ten or fifteen degrees closer to the wind. We were converging on Swedish Match, gaining both bearing and range. And doing it from far enough to leeward that they couldn't block the overtaking lane with the disturbed air off their sails. If the breeze stayed up above twenty knots we could catch them. Swedish Match desperately hung on to her bigger sail hoping for the opposite. If she could avoid the sail change, she could hold us off at the headland. We were almost willing the breeze to stay up, nine days of exhausting yacht racing completely forgotten. And every minute that it did, we got a metre or two closer.

The breeze did hold up, even increased, and on Swedish Match they cracked, changing down to a smaller fractional asymmetric. It wasn't a good sail change either: they sagged a little closer. We had the edge now, both in speed and mentally. And over the next couple of hours, as the two boats thundered around Point Perpendicular, we slowly ground past. We had a half-mile lead. The atmosphere on the boat was completely charged. But we already had another crucial decision to make. The course to Sydney was twenty degrees further offwind – we could hold a bigger spinnaker as we bore away. We thought we could afford to wait for Swedish Match to make their move first. We were wrong.

The A9 was a slightly smaller spinnaker, it had got us up in front of Swedish Match and we were still going a little closer to the wind – faster too, but slowly sailing up off their course. This time we went with the A5.5. It was another perfect change, and another good call. Down below Rudi plotted us back in front of Swedish Match with a slightly increased lead. It was a done deal, the tight ball of tension bouncing around my stomach started to unravel, just a fraction. With the day and the mileage dropping away,

the sun was setting, the wind was easing and going back to the south from the south-east.

BANG!

The response was instant, no one even bothered to shout. We could all see the problem. The tack had blown off the spinnaker. The front of the sail ripped off the pole and blew like a flag out the back of the boat. EF Language came off her rails and hit the brakes. But the A6 was packed and ready and everyone was already moving. It was dark, blowing almost thirty knots. Finding the right rope and leading it to the right place – clear of fouls and tangles, under pressure from the charging boat behind and from the afterguard – was no easy job. But Curtis and Juggy knew every inch of the boat, and with Josh co-ordinating from the middle the recovery was peerless.

The spinnaker take-down line was run. Josh hitched it up to the weather primary winch, vacated by the now slack guy that ran to the broken tack fitting. The halyard smoked, handles spun and arms gathered the broken sail to bundle it below. The spinnaker gear was unclipped and rerun to the bow. The hoist was clean, the sock came off perfectly, with good trim out of the set and almost instant reacceleration. We knew we were still in the lead, because we could see their bow navigation light about three boat lengths off our stern. It was all on again.

Then came Rudi's voice out of the hatch. 'She's still over three-quarters of a mile away, boys. Good job on deck.'

'Rudi, you sure about that? She looks about four feet off our transom!' was the disbelieving response.

CONSTANT HANDLING OF WET ROPES CAN HAVE A BRUTAL EFFECT ON HANDS.

'Three-quarters of a mile and we're gaining.'

The A6 was a bigger sail, and as the wind continued to drop and swing behind us it became the right sail. But it was hugely loaded in the stiff breeze, and there was only one masthead sail left: the A5.3, which no one likes. Don't ask me why, we just hate it. It was readied for a quick hoist anyway, but we were really on edge that the A6 didn't blow.

The miles ticked by, disturbed only by shouts of 'trim' and 'stop'; the crash of the handles and whirr of the winches; moans from the heavily loaded structure of the boat. Time was trickling away for Swedish Match and she had to do something. Still with a smaller spinnaker up, she started to sail closer to the wind. We couldn't match her with the big masthead, and were forced to let her gain the separation. But the wind was still dropping and lifting. Sailors have a saying that 'What goes up, must come back down'. Swedish Match gained distance towards us as she climbed higher, but not enough, and when she was finally forced to point back at Sydney Heads, changing to the big masthead spinnaker at the same time, we had pulled clear ahead to almost a three-mile lead.

The dice had one final roll: Sydney Harbour. Anything could happen inside the high walls of headlands and houses. We prepared everything we could think of, and a couple that we could only dream about. The sail stack on deck was completely reorganised, with a selection of lighter air, upwind, reaching and running sails pulled clear. The half-ounce spinnaker, the big R3 and R1 reachers and the J2 headsail were on top. The rest of the sails were carefully packed down below so they could be found quickly. Speed of response to the changing conditions was more important than the extra kilos on deck.

And the conditions did change. Clouds built up behind us and Swedish Match came pouring in towards us on the new pressure – just as we fell into lighter air under South Head. Rudi counted down the miles and as Paul called for the gybe into the harbour entrance, they were only a mile and a half behind. We didn't need it. It had been a long day, and we'd done the job. But like it or not, there were seven miles to go and the pressure was still on. We carried the spinnaker for another mile and a half, before heading up for the finish line. We had changed to a reaching headsail just as the spectator fleet spotted us.

It was just in time. The world went crazy. Nine days – so focused and so intense, with just ourselves, the schedules and the occasional email for company. And suddenly there were people everywhere. The whole boat was illuminated in a pool of light for the television cameras. Our carefully acquired night vision disappeared in an instant. Boats swarmed around us and the radar was cluttered with returns; the blip that was Swedish Match disappeared in the deluge as quickly as her navigation light. We were blindly groping our way towards the finish with no idea of where the opposition was. It was desperately tense, awful.

The only good thing was that there was a tight reaching angle to the line. EF Language kept her bow up and her head down and charged for the finish as hard as she could in the lightening breeze. We talked about another change, but held off – we'd lose too much, it was better to hang on. And slowly the lights of the Opera House appeared out of the night. The famous white sails of the roof soared over the gathered spectators. Flares lit up a night filled with Team EF flags. And only then did we believe it was going to be all right and succumbed to a tidal wave of pure joy. It was relief that we'd felt in Cape Town. Relief that we could be competitive. That we hadn't committed years of our lives to a project that had somewhere taken a wrong turn. But Sydney was joy, joy at winning a tough race that was fought inch by inch. There's no other feeling like it.

In the end the first seven boats finished within twenty-six minutes of each other: a big difference in points and emotion for a tiny amount of time. All nine boats finished within an hour and a half, they queued up in Darling Harbour for their turn on the medal podium. It was the tightest finish in the history of the Whitbread, an incredible end to an incident-strewn leg. Second-placed Swedish Match and fifth-placed Innovation Kvaerner both buckled the base of their mast but managed to keep them in the boat, although Frostad's team on Innovation Kvaerner was forced to anchor and get spares from a helicopter. They also lost bowman Alby Pratt overboard in the Bass Strait, but picked him up within seven minutes.

The only dark spot on a glorious Sydney welcome was that EF Education, after holding sixth or seventh for much of the leg, had been edged out in the power and stability-dominated conditions of the final day. They collected their first last-place finish. And Anna had been hurt when a winch drum sheered off its base only two hours after the start. Her hand had been heavily strapped, and she had only been able to call trim, not change it. But she had still stood her watches, working with her one good hand. The day after the finish, X-rays established that Keryn's on-board assessment had been right: Anna's hand was broken.

93

NEXT PAGE: THE DOWNWIND START IN FREMANTLE.

EF LANGUAGE PASSES WILSON'S PROMONTORY JUST BEFORE ENGAGING IN HER DESPERATE BATTLE TO THE FINISH WITH

SWEDISH MATCH. CLOSING ON SYDNEY WITH AN ADEQUATE, BUT NOT SAFE, LEAD OVER SWEDISH MATCH.

NEXT PAGE: EF LANGUAGE SLIPS ACROSS THE LINE IN FRONT OF THE SYDNEY OPERA HOUSE, JUST SIX MINUTES AHEAD.

THE CLOCK KEEPER

Leg Four: even shorter than the third leg, 1,270 nautical miles across the Tasman Sea from Sydney to Auckland. And EF Language once again won the start, leading the charge out of Sydney harbour. But within hours of getting out into open ocean the weather started to play games with the fleet. First a trough, then a tiny low-pressure system made a mockery of the weather forecast. For EF Education, the gains and losses became irrelevant when the headsail tack fitting broke and they were forced to run north to repair it. Things were hardly going any better for EF Language. After positioning to the north, they found themselves bounced to the back of the fleet as the low pressure formed and the south gained the advantage. By Day Three, they had been forced to lose a lot of miles to swop sides and move south, hoping to take advantage of more breeze and a better sailing angle as the low pressure moved away to the north. But it was a painful three days and the 18.00 GMT schedule had put them in eighth place.

Magnus:

Rudi had woken me when the midnight GMT schedule came in. Not deliberately, but I'd heard talking and something in my subconscious had told me what was going on. The previous schedule had been bad enough, and we'd continued south for a good couple of hours after that before we had finally tacked to starboard and headed for Cape Reinga at the northern tip of New Zealand. So with only about four hours on the better tack, it was unreasonable to expect any gains – yet. It would take a day or so for the strategy to work. If the strategy worked. The schedule was almost encouraging. We had gained a place, up to seventh now, but we were still a full sixty-two nautical miles behind the leader, Swedish Match. She was forty-nine points behind us overall, and that meant we needed to get up to at least fifth to hold our overall lead. I lay back in the bunk and stared at the deckhead. It was hard to understand our situation after the start from Sydney,

102

when we had sailed into such a comfortable lead so quickly. I kept telling myself that these kinds of reversals were the real test of the Whitbread; you had to bounce back from them as quickly as you could. But if the south didn't pay off on the way into Cape Reinga, then we were in deep trouble.

I rolled upright in the bunk; there was no way I could get back to sleep. Paul was on deck and Rudi was hidden away in the navigation station. Everyone else had slept through the schedule. It was totally quiet, except for the sounds of the boat: the crisp gurgle of water from the forefoot; the hum from Rudi's electrical toys; a groan from a straining sheet on deck. I sat listening, trying to take pleasure from just being out there, at sea. It wasn't happening; I wanted to be winning. I glanced at the clock on the bulkhead above the galley. It was almost 10.30 in the morning – ship's time. I wasn't back on watch until 14.00 –three and a half hours away.

Ship's time was my responsibility as the clock keeper for EF Language. I had to adjust the onboard clocks, one in the galley and one on deck, so that the ship's time kept up with local time as we moved east around the world. If we didn't adjust the ship's clock, then breakfast would slowly work its way towards dinner, and we would end up eating dinner as the sun rose and this kind of thing throws the body's internal clock into a spin. For every fifteen degrees of longit-

ude that we travelled east, the clock had to go forward one hour. In the Southern Ocean – when you are doing 400-nautical-mile days – that can mean changing the clock every day. But for this leg, with only twenty-three degrees of longitude difference between Sydney and Auckland, we could get away with changing the clock just once. The question was, on which day should the clocks go forward?

The time of the change was simple enough – it was always done at 11.30 in the morning, when the clocks would go forward an hour to 12.30 in the afternoon. Since 12.00 noon was the time of one of our watch changes, that meant the on-watch coming down early, and the off-watch going up early. So both of those watches were treated equally, they both lost half an hour's sleep and half an hour on deck. But the alternate watch (under the Swedish system), that changed at 14.00 on that day, would work or sleep right through the clock's being moved forward. So they would either lose an hour's sleep or lose an hour's work. Whether your watch was changing at 12.00 or 14.00 depended on which day it was in the four-day cycle of the watch system, as did whether you lost an hour's sleep or an hour's work if you were on the 14.00 change.

Confused? You should be. So are most of the crew, especially when they're tired. The complexity of the system, combined with the element of winners and losers, makes the clock keeper's a contentious position. Particularly on a slow and short leg like this one, when I could choose almost any day to change the clock. That's why I got the job. It was partly because I'd done it before, but mostly because, as the oldest on the boat, I could wield a master-mariner-like authority over grumpy crewmen! So far, I hadn't done the change. Perhaps today should be the day. We were only about 250 nautical miles from Cape Reinga, and then it was mostly south, not east, to Auckland. I decided to worry about it later. In the meantime, I thought it was about my turn to do something really useful – pump the bilge out.

I hauled myself out of the bunk, hit the deck, then braced myself against a sudden movement as the boat lurched off a wave. The remains of the breakfast dishes glowered at me from the galley. I would do those first. Although many of the jobs and responsibilities in the daily routine of the boat were rigorously assigned, there were a few that weren't – pumping out the bilge and washing the dishes amongst them. Although Stevie was responsible for the food, and he had a real clean-up every few days, the few dishes that were produced at each meal time were everyone's concern. And I hadn't done either the dishes or the bilge since the start of the leg. I was awake, had some time to burn, and now was an ideal moment to take my turn.

I pumped a little sea water into the bowl and pulled the soapy sponge out of the pile of dishes. I wiped it over them and scraped at the redried freeze-dried as best I could, before piling them in the rack. It wasn't much of a clean, and if anyone got sick it went round the crew pretty quickly. But we just couldn't afford the weight of the gas and diesel to wash up in hot, fresh water every day. I had just about finished when Juggy slid down the hatch, mumbled good morning, and disappeared aft. I watched briefly until I realised he was checking the foils for weed. We had a special optical instrument, an endoscope, that allowed us to see the rudder, keel and propeller through tiny lenses fitted into the skin of the hull. Any amount of weed or plastic wrapped around the foils was enough to slow the boat down – never mind the huge chunks that float around in some parts of the world. It was another of those jobs that had to be done by everyone, all the time.

I finished the dishes and pumped the sink dry, then went forward to check the bow compartment for water. I found it wasn't too bad, but it would still be worth getting the bilge pump out to dry her properly. The whole team, crew and shore support, had worked incredibly hard at waterproofing the boat. There was very little that came down the mast partners, or through screw holes and fittings. But some water always got in through the hatches during sail changes, and more found its way through the halyard sheaves and into the mast from where it trickled out of the bottom of the mast butt. I came back aft just in

'FOR EVERY FIFTEEN DEGREES OF LONGITUDE THAT WE TRAVELLED EAST, THE CLOCK HAD TO GO FORWARD ONE HOUR.'

THE DAILY DOMESTIC AND MAINTENANCE WORK MUST BE COMPLETED BY THE CREW WHEN THEY ARE OFF WATCH,
ERODING THEIR REST PERIOD, BUT LEAVING THE WATCH ON DECK TO RACE THE BOAT WITHOUT DISTRACTION.

time to hear Juggy yell upstairs that the foils were clear. I was flipping the inspection hatch off the floorboards to get at the bilge pump as he turned from the companionway.

'Magnus, my breakfast felt like it was at lunchtime. When are you going to change the clock?' he said.

I turned round and smiled. 'Maybe today.'

'Good.' Then he hesitated, starting to frown. 'Maybe not. I've got a pile of media stuff to do. I don't need to lose the hour.'

'That is so typical – no one can ever make their minds up about when I should do it.'

Juggy grunted. 'Doesn't make any difference, since you go right ahead and do it when you want anyway,' he said as he slid into the seat at the media station.

The media station consisted of a video editing facility, and satellite communications equipment to send the footage he shot to the Race Office. From there it went on to television stations in Sweden and around the world. It took up a lot of Juggy's time – often out of his off-watch time when he should have been asleep. But on this occasion he was fortunate, going upwind there wasn't too much sailing to do on deck.

I have a rule never to argue about the clock, so I went back to the electrical bilge pump. It's stored under the floorboards forward, with a five-metre hose that you run around the boat like a vacuum cleaner. Sometimes it's quicker just to bail and sponge the water out of the worst places, but I had the time for a thorough job. When I finished it was eleven o'clock. Decision time – clocks forward or not? I ought to do it, we had done enough distance east. I made my mind up and yelled up on deck, 'Clocks forward today. Half

an hour to watch change.' There were smiles, at least someone was happy. Now I had to wake the new watch, sleeping like babies. They probably weren't going to be so chuffed.

I wound the clocks forward first, then I shook Curtis awake, and Klabbe and Marco. 'On deck in half an hour, guys,' I said, seeing Curtis check the watch on his wrist. I knew what was coming.

'Oh no, Magnus, don't do it today, I really need the sleep.'

'I keep trying to explain to you guys that it doesn't make any difference. You lose a half-hour off both the watch and off your sleep.'

'And I keep telling you I need the sleep. Do it tomorrow.'

'By tomorrow we'll be eating lunch by moonlight,' retorted Crusty, who'd stuck his head down the hatch from on deck to check the food was on and the new watch was being woken.

'You would say that, you're the one who'll lose an hour off your watch if he does it today.' This was Stevie; we shared a watch. And the watch that went up at 14.00 got the worst of the deal.

Crusty just smiled and said, 'You'll do the lunch, Magnus?' and when I nodded he disappeared out of the hatch.

But Stevie wasn't finished, 'Hey, you think it's bad for you guys – I just lost a whole hour of sleep.' He scowled at Curtis, before rolling over and pulling the sleeping bag over his head.

Curtis looked at me, I looked at him, and we both shrugged. Like I said, there's winners and losers.

'Don't forget to tell Rudi, he has a hard enough job

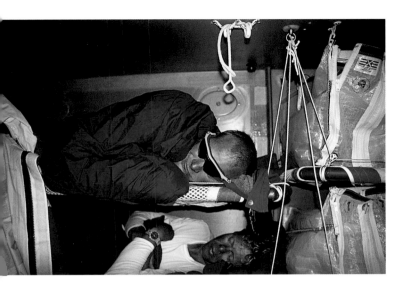

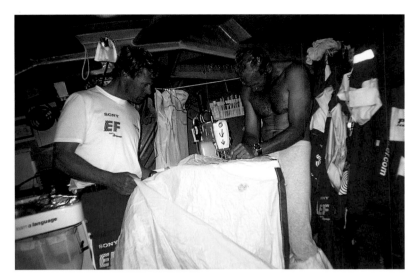

remembering anyway,' Marco added quietly, as he slid out of the bunk. Both Rudi and Paul 'floated' – they weren't part of the watch system, so they tended to live on GMT (Greenwich Mean Time), the time back in England that all the weather forecast and position report schedules used. The trouble came when Rudi was asked to wake the off-watch, and he was an hour slow on ship's time. Then people got grumpy because they were woken late for their watch. Time – it's a killer, I tell you.

I set about the final job for the morning – putting some water on for lunch. That would save someone coming down from the deck. We ate at each of the watch changes, prepared a half-hour before, either by someone on deck, or someone who had to be woken up early from the new watch. Occasionally Rudi or Paul would do it. But not this time, they had too much to worry about with the weather. I put the water on and dug around amongst the food bags for lunch. The bags were small, white holdalls, they only held two-days' food each, so that they could be moved easily to keep the trim of the boat correct. But it was a major job to keep the current bag somewhere near the top of the pile so that we could find it.

However, I found the right bag quickly enough and pulled out lunch; two packets of freeze-dried pasta. I smiled, because another of the endless list of routine jobs that kept the boat running smoothly was being done efficiently. There was Stevie on the food; Curt checked and maintained the winches and deck gear; Marco did the sails; while I was responsible for the rig. Klabbe and Josh ran all the boat systems, checking the battery charge and running the generator to keep it topped up. Then there was the making of drinking water, which we did up to three times a day, so that we carried as little weight in water as possible. It was a wonder we had any time for sailing. That was the whole point really: the better the organisation, the more time you had to sail and sleep. Sailing and sleeping won the race, and the tidier and more disciplined the boat's living routine, the better chance you had to win. Just seeing it all happening around me made me feel good again. We might be down at the moment, but we would come through. The fundamentals were all in place.

And come through they did. The southern side paid dividends as the fleet approached Cape Reinga on starboard tack. At the headland the leader, Swedish Match, sailed into a huge wind hole and stopped. Four boats sailed past her, including EF Language, which moved into a fourth place that she held to the finish. Kiwi skipper Grant Dalton brought Merit Cup home first in front of the home crowd, followed by Toshiba and Chessie Racing. After EF Language, Swedish Match held her fifth place from Silk Cut, Innovation Kvaerner and BrunelSunergy, while EF Education struggled in with her broken tack fitting, in last place.

Toshiba's co-skipper Dennis Conner launched a protest against EF Language for not showing navigation lights at night, then flew home to the United States. The protest was dismissed for being filed incorrectly. The results maintained EF Language's overall lead – now held over Merit Cup. And the whole fleet got down to the serious business of preparing for Leg Five. Back into the Southern Ocean, where Magnus and his crew-mates had some unfinished business.

EF LANGUAGE APPROACHES THE FINISH LINE IN AUCKLAND IN BRIGHT SUNSHINE.

EIGHT HOURS AFTER EF LANGUAGE, HER SISTER SHIP ARRIVES IN DARKNESS AND RAIN.

THE MAST

113

The fifth leg – 6,670 nautical miles from Auckland to São Sebastião – presented the greatest single challenge of the 1997/98 Whitbread Race. This is acknowledged by the scoring system (which determines the points for each place on the basis of both length and likely conditions on each leg) as it carries the highest points total of any leg. Though it is not the longest, it has the greatest mix of the most demanding conditions. Traversing first the stormy Southern Ocean before rounding Cape Horn and heading north into the unpredictable weather conditions, heat and currents of the east coast of South America, it is the ultimate test of the fleet's racing and sailing qualities. But for EF Language, Leg Five had come to represent even more. By their own admission, and by widespread perception, they had failed at the challenge of the Southern Ocean in Leg Two. Now they were going back, and this time, it was personal.

But the start, amongst the throng of Auckland's supporters and well-wishers, could not have been more different. Once again the fleet struggled south in light air, crawling into the Southern Ocean. EF Language was with the leading pack of six boats that dived south early to make the running. Holding to the north were Innovation Kvaerner and EF Education, awaiting a tiny storm cell of low pressure that was swirling up off the tip of New Zealand from where it would hunt down the fleet. Late on February 6 it struck. The boats to the south were pounded with violent headwinds for ten hours, while Innovation Kvaerner saw sixty-eight knots on her beam. EF Education was only a little further from the centre.

Anna:

The previous watch had been a nightmare. The wind had kicked in hard, and we had broached while preparing to gybe with a reaching headsail and the staysail. The staysail had come down in pieces and the headsail had flogged out of the luff groove, before the halyard broke. We had just about got it sorted by the end of my watch, and had put the storm jib up, with a couple of reefs in the mainsail, while we waited for the low-pressure system to go through to the south of us. We had gybed to starboard just before I went below. Night was coming on quickly, and we were flying east in a south-westerly breeze, which was pushing up to forty knots and more. I had crawled into my bunk completely exhausted, having just about managed to peel off my oilskins. But as always it was a terrible struggle to get to sleep with the boat pounding through the waves at such a pace. The low pressure had gone through so quickly, rotating

the wind from north to west and then south, that it had left the ocean hopelessly confused. The waves came from all directions, and in the dark it was impossible to ease the boat's passage through them. With each crash and jolt I half woke, bracing myself against the new motion.

The critical wave woke me as we screamed up the back of it, pushing half the ocean past my ear, mere inches away through the boat's thin Kevlar skin. Then there was an ominous silence as we launched off the back face like some huge, psychotic Hawaiian windsurfer. I drifted off my bunk as the hull became airborne, grabbing for a handhold to set against the landing. It was a nauseating crash as we came down, but for a few precious seconds the thunder of noise seemed normal. Then the boat threw itself into the wind, the sails flogged and I heard the shouts from on deck even over the sail roar. I guessed what had happened. The boat was coming into the wind to unload the mast – something on the rig must have failed as we smacked back into the ocean.

As the crew on deck worked to drop the mainsail, those of us down below struggled to find our gear. Bodies and clothing were flying everywhere as the hull lurched and rolled crazily, hammered by wind and waves. By the time I hauled myself through the hatch the mainsail was half down, cascading onto the deck in folds of heavy, wet Kevlar. I fought my way past it,

straight into the spray that was lashing the boat from all angles. The boat was rolling completely unpredictably in the confused seas. Someone was yelling in my ear, 'The D2's gone. We've got to tack as soon as the mainsail's down. Grab the runner.' The D2 was a diagonal support rod that ran from the outboard end of the first spreader to the inboard end of the second. Without it, the mast would crumple and fold under the force of its own sail load and rig tension. We were very lucky the mast was still up there at all. Only lightning reactions on the helm and mainsheet had saved it.

Those were my thoughts as I battled across the deck aft towards the runner winch. As the final roll of mainsail came down, the storm jib was backed. The head of the boat paid off on to port tack, then swung away on to a run under the urging of the rudder. Going downwind with just the storm jib up was a huge contrast to the violence and chaos of the mainsail drop. The boat still rolled brutally, but it did so in a seemingly surreal silence. We folded and lashed the mainsail to the boom. With torches on the rig we could see the broken rod flapping from the second spreader. Bridget and Lisa were already preparing to go aloft. We hoisted them up there, and at first they tried to rethread the rod on to the turnbuckle.

In fact the thread was completely stripped, but it took them a while to see that – twenty feet off the deck, rolling gunwale to gunwale in the black night of a

'WE HAD JUST ABOUT GOT IT SORTED BY THE END OF MY WATCH ...'

Southern Ocean gale. When they finally gave up on the repair to await daylight, we rigged a jury D2. A rope, twisted for tension, was run around the second spreader root at the mast and tied down to the outboard end of the first spreader in place of the broken D2. With that tightened and in place, we gybed back on to the weakened starboard side, and once again headed east towards the Horn. Below, Lynnath was on the satellite communications system, telling the world what had happened.

When the report arrived from the boat, at both the Race Office in Southampton and at Team EF's base in Gothenburg, there was instant activity. Next of kin must be informed before anything else can be done – no one wants to hear that their loved ones are in trouble in a television bulletin. A release was prepared by the press team of Georgina Hyde in England and Marika Hjelm in Sweden, to be sent to the world's media as soon as the families had been told. Meanwhile Project Director Johan Salén was concentrating on arrangements for repairing the broken rigging. He contacted the team's mast expert, Dave White, who had just finished helping to pack up the shore support facility in Auckland. As more information came

through the satellite link from the boat, the repair seemed straightforward: a new rod and fastenings, with some modifications, could be sent out and put in place.

The biggest question was where to send the equipment. The nearest land was the Chatham Islands, only 800 nautical miles behind the boat to the west. The team's meteorologist, Roger Badham, was the next to be brought into the loop – but his forecast was not good. The islands would be upwind, through heavy weather and big seas. The weakened rig almost certainly wouldn't take the pounding of extended upwind sailing. The decision was taken aboard EF Education to carry on eastwards to Ushuaia in Argentina, just north of Cape Horn – the southernmost city in the world. Dave White would arrange for the new rod and fastenings to be sent to meet them there. Back on board, the girls had improved their jury rig and hoisted a trysail with the coming of daylight, and continued east.

After the D2 broke, we all knew that this leg was over for us, one way or the other. When something like that happens it takes a moment or two to assess the damage, then you just instinctively start trying to

make the situation safe. It was only when we had the jury rig settled and were heading for Cape Horn again that what had happened sank in. Everyone was very quiet for a day or so; it was desperately disappointing. I think that we had wanted to prove ourselves on this leg more than any other. But as the days went by we settled into some kind of a routine. We made a deck of cards out of scraps of sailcloth. We slept, and read the few books on board – mostly the equipment manuals! With four on deck at a time, and working only a three-hour watch with six hours off, boredom was the biggest problem.

Even on watch, there wasn't much to do. We didn't dare trim the boat too hard, and couldn't use spinnakers. So with just a headsail up, and often a storm jib, it was a matter of swopping between the trysail and the mainsail, and pulling reefs in and out. The weather systems came and went, but by February 16 there was a big low-pressure coming in from the southwest, with winds forecast at fifty knots or more. We were limping eastwards on the good port gybe, in the northerly flow off its front edge, watching the breeze build, going as fast as we could to try and avoid the incoming gale. We had the storm jib up and two reefs in the main. I was on watch, sitting back, thinking that soon we should change down to the trysail. The sun was crawling up in a grey sky – a little more

light and I would suggest it to the others.

It's different when you are on deck. You hear the bang, and by the time you look up – struggling to find a view out of the foul-weather jacket hood – the mast is in the water. It's instant – full and certain knowledge of the worst possible occurrence. You have the rig down in the Southern Ocean, and you're sitting helplessly in the path of a fifty-knot storm. We already knew our leg was over, now it could be the whole race. But again, you forget all that and just react to the situation. And the situation was that the mast was broken at the first and second spreader from our second failed D2. Worse, it was hanging over the side and pounding the living daylights out of the hull. That's the most terrifying prospect, that the mast will saw or hammer its way through the boat. Then you are in real trouble. We had to clear the damage, and fast.

The mess was almost incomprehensible: rope, wire and frayed metal strewn about the boat, tossed there like some giant, fuzzy ball of swarf. But the immediate priority was clear, to get the rig lashed into the side of the hull to stop it pounding. The crew below were up on deck in a moment. One group worked aft, trying to strap the mast to the transom, another group forward. It took about twenty minutes to stop the mast moving. The next step was to get the main-

117

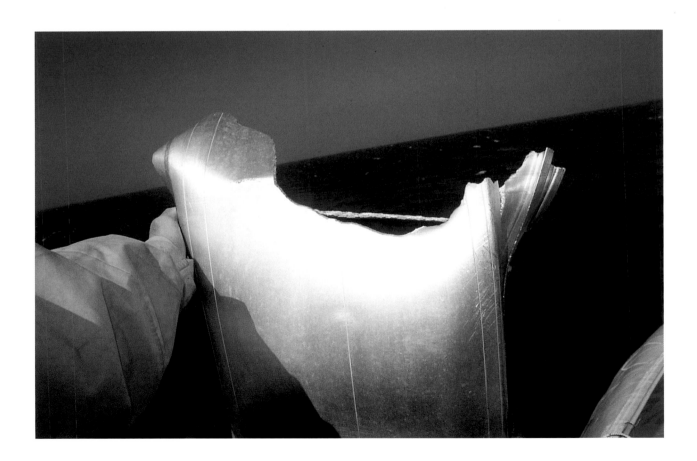

'THE MESS WAS ALMOST INCOMPREHENSIBLE: ROPE, WIRE AND FRAYED METAL STREWN ABOUT THE BOAT.'

SÃO SEBASTIÃO

sail down from the stump, where it was still catching the wind and exacerbating the motion of the boat. And the breeze was building, ominous grey clouds pouring in from the west. The daylight helped, but seeing those clouds and the big rollers coming in certainly didn't. The webbing was cut to detach the mainsail from the halyard, and the sail pulled down the three shattered sections of the mast. With the storm jib retrieved from the water, we were ready to try and lift the rig on to the deck.

The wind was howling. With our wind instruments two metres under water we had no way of knowing quite how bad it was, but it looked every bit of the fifty knots forecast. The breeze was whipping spray across the boat with a ferocity that made it impossible to look upwind. It stung face and hands, rattled into foul-weather gear with an intensity that could knock your breath away. With the mast dragging in the water and holding the hull beam-on to the sea, waves simply rolled over the deck. It was constantly awash, making it difficult enough to hold on, let alone work. We used the harnesses to brace ourselves in place and did the best we could with one hand.

We lashed ropes around the mast, then made them up on to the winches. And because the mast was solid, we could use the jockey pole and the spinnaker pole to lever it up. That, combined with timing the heave

so that the roll of the boat helped us, finally got the mast on to the deck. The third and fourth spreaders had to come off to get it to lay flat. The time went incredibly quickly, so concentrated was the effort, but it took almost six hours to make the mast secure. It was another two hours before we had set up the mast for a jury rig, by tying a rope backstay and forestay from the top of the stump to the bow and transom. Then halyards were rigged through blocks at the new top of the mast, and the trysail was hoisted sideways, with the foot as the luff. I put another tack eye in the storm jib, so that it would fit the shortened fore-triangle. And finally we had steerage way again, and could start moving towards Cape Horn.

It was a big relief, but only a small mercy. The motion of the boat with such a small rig was horrendous – and the speed worse. Previously we had at least had sail changes to do, now there was nothing. The first few days we fiddled a little with the jury rig – using the boom rather than just an aft pad-eye to sheet the trysail; squaring the storm jib out with a spinnaker pole when we were running. We tried to keep ourselves busy with other things: making work lists, pulling fittings that we could use again off the damaged rig – and the cards came back out. But that was it. There was nothing else but desolate ocean and a crippled yacht that shuddered and juddered and

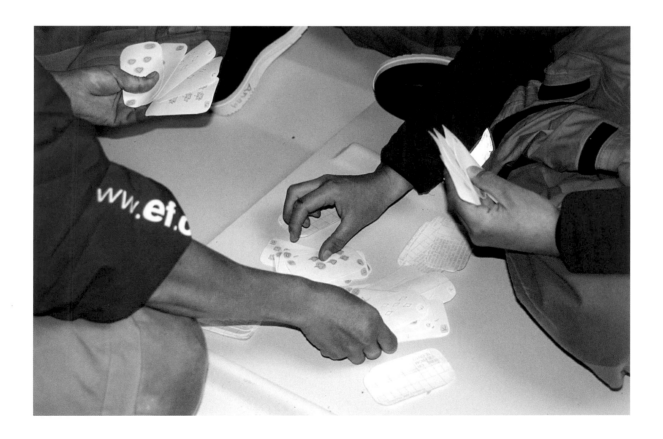

'PREVIOUSLY WE HAD AT LEAST HAD SAIL CHANGES TO DO, NOW THERE WAS NOTHING.'

SÃO SEBASTIÃO

wobbled so badly you couldn't stand up below. Days with nothing to do except wonder about our race; the prospects if the weather got bad and we had to go upwind; and the chances of being ready for the restart.

The total loss of the mast also required a response of a higher order from the shore team. The initial moves were now practised – contacting next-of-kin and issuing a statement to the press. But the problem of repairing or replacing the mast was vastly different to just sending a new D2 to Ushuaia. Johan Salén tackled the problem head on with every resource he could lay his hands on. Digital photos of the damage were transmitted from the boat and emailed to Dave White for analysis. The diagnosis was swift: beyond repair. Team EF's spare mast, lying in Lymington, England, would have to be transported to the boat.

The first problem was how to guarantee that EF Education didn't end up sitting becalmed off South America, without enough diesel to make it into port. Or worse, as the girls feared, being blown on to the Chilean or Argentine coast without the sail power or diesel to go upwind and claw to safety. Former Whitbread skipper Skip Novak knew the Commodore at the Ushuaia Yacht Club (membership five boats) who had a contact in the Chilean Navy. They offered to stand by to tow the crippled yacht – for free – should she get into trouble. That was a start, now all they had to do was get the mast to the boat.

A thorough check of the shipping companies established that there was nothing leaving Europe that would arrive in South America in time. Instead, the mast would have to be flown – but an eighty-five-foot mast isn't something you can just check in as excess baggage. The Royal Air Force didn't have a plane big enough to get it to the Falklands. It could go as air freight in two pieces to Buenos Aires or São Paulo, but how to get the mast to the boat (or vice versa) from there in the short time before the start of Leg Six? Private jets couldn't load it normally, and a plan to push it in through the hole created by a removed windscreen was scuppered when the civil aviation authorities demanded that the aircraft be completely pressure-tested – after the mast was loaded and the windscreen replaced.

Other options were considered. Team EF sponsor Cool Carriers offered to divert a boat to Ushuaia to meet EF Education and load the yacht, taking her to the mast in Buenos Aires. It was risky, because the crane facilities in Ushuaia were uncertain, and a cradle would have to be built locally. Alternatively the ship could have towed the yacht – but that was potentially dangerous were the weather to get bad. Trucking the mast the 3,800 kilometres from Buenos Aires to Ushuaia also looked to be impossible in the time available. Then the Argentine Air Force came to the rescue. They agreed to charter out one of their Hercules aircraft to fly the mast from Buenos Aires to Ushuaia. The spar would have to be cut in two, but Dave White could fly to Ushuaia and resplice and rig the mast.

The plan worked, but only just. The women safely rounded a stormy Cape Horn and moved into calmer waters in the lee of the Argentine coast. There they finally started the engine with the diesel they had so carefully conserved. They were met by Johan in an old pilot boat and towed the final twenty-five nautical miles to Ushuaia, through the stunning scenery of the Beagle Channel. They arrived at midnight on February 25, and were greeted by twelve young girls who sang songs of welcome, with a red rose for each of the crew. Meanwhile, Dave White flew from São Sebastião, where he had arranged a repair kit and tools, to Buenos Aires, to meet the mast.

All was almost lost at the final moment – the Hercules was on call for United Nations duty should Kofi Annan fail to secure a last-minute agreement on weapons inspections in Iraq. But Saddam Hussein gave way and the plane was cleared for the charter. Dave White saw the mast onto the Hercules and flew down with it – sitting on his courtesy parachute, because it was the only soft object in the aircraft. He touched down to an ecstatic welcome from the crew – now happily cleaned up and well rested. They would need the rest. It was a frantic three days' work to clear away the damage, prepare the new rig, repair sails and reprovision. They worked twenty-hour days, surrounded by the mountain snows, peaks and glaciers of Patagonia. The people of Ushuaia were fantastic, on-hand at every turn to provide help – tools, lights, food and shelter. And at 04.00 on February 28 EF Education left for the 2,100 nautical mile journey to São Sebastião. She continued to race for another five and a half days, before a combination of light air, storms, and the already damaged mainsail failing again, forced the crew to start the engine and – since it was no longer an emergency – retire. It was a tremendously valiant effort to collect the points for eighth place. But in the end the priority was to get to São Sebastião for the restart.

119

FOLLOWING PAGES: MAKING THE BROKEN MAST SAFE AND ARRANGING A JURY RIG TOOK THE CREW OF EF EDUCATION EIGHT HOURS.

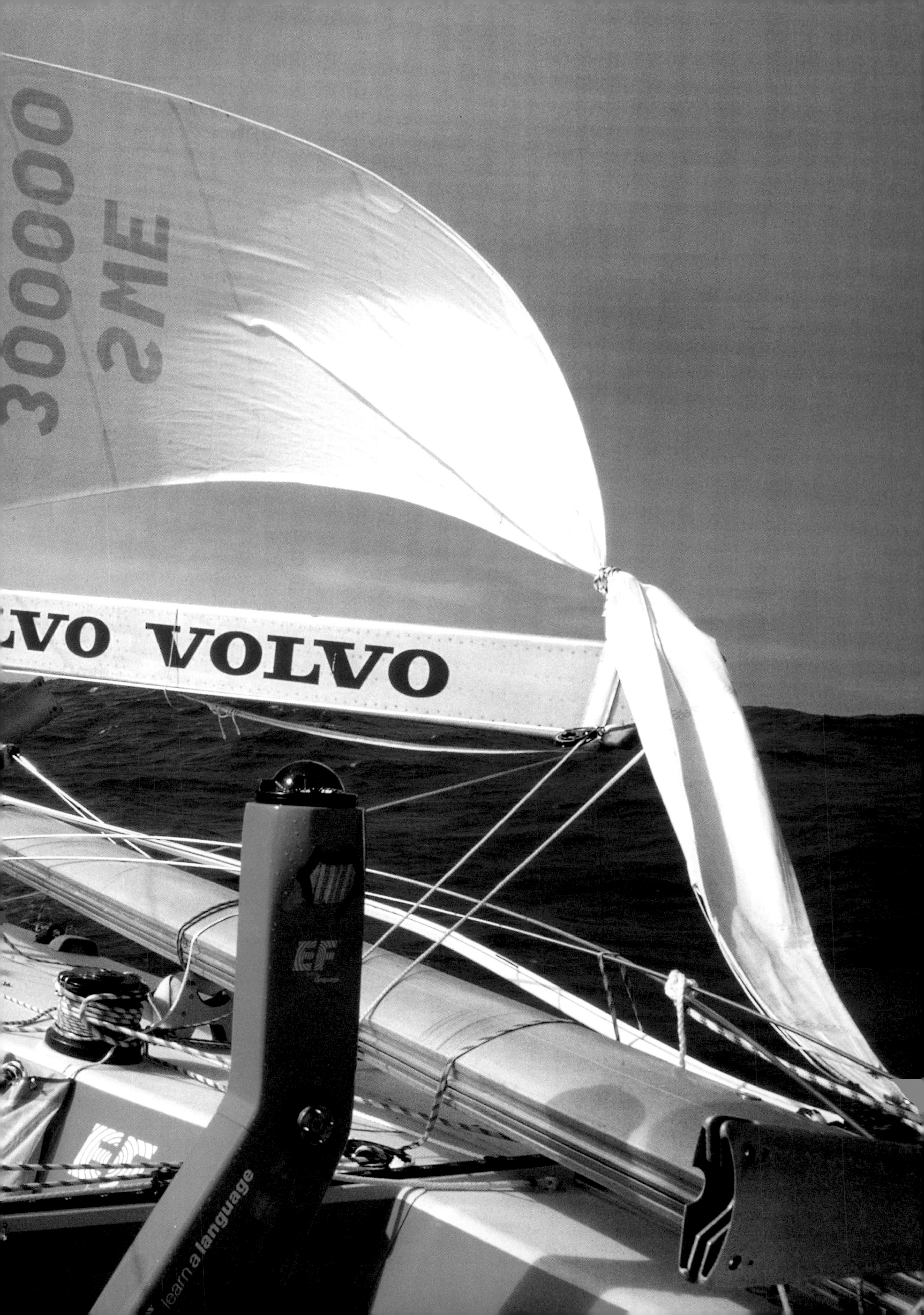
LVO VOLVO
learn a language

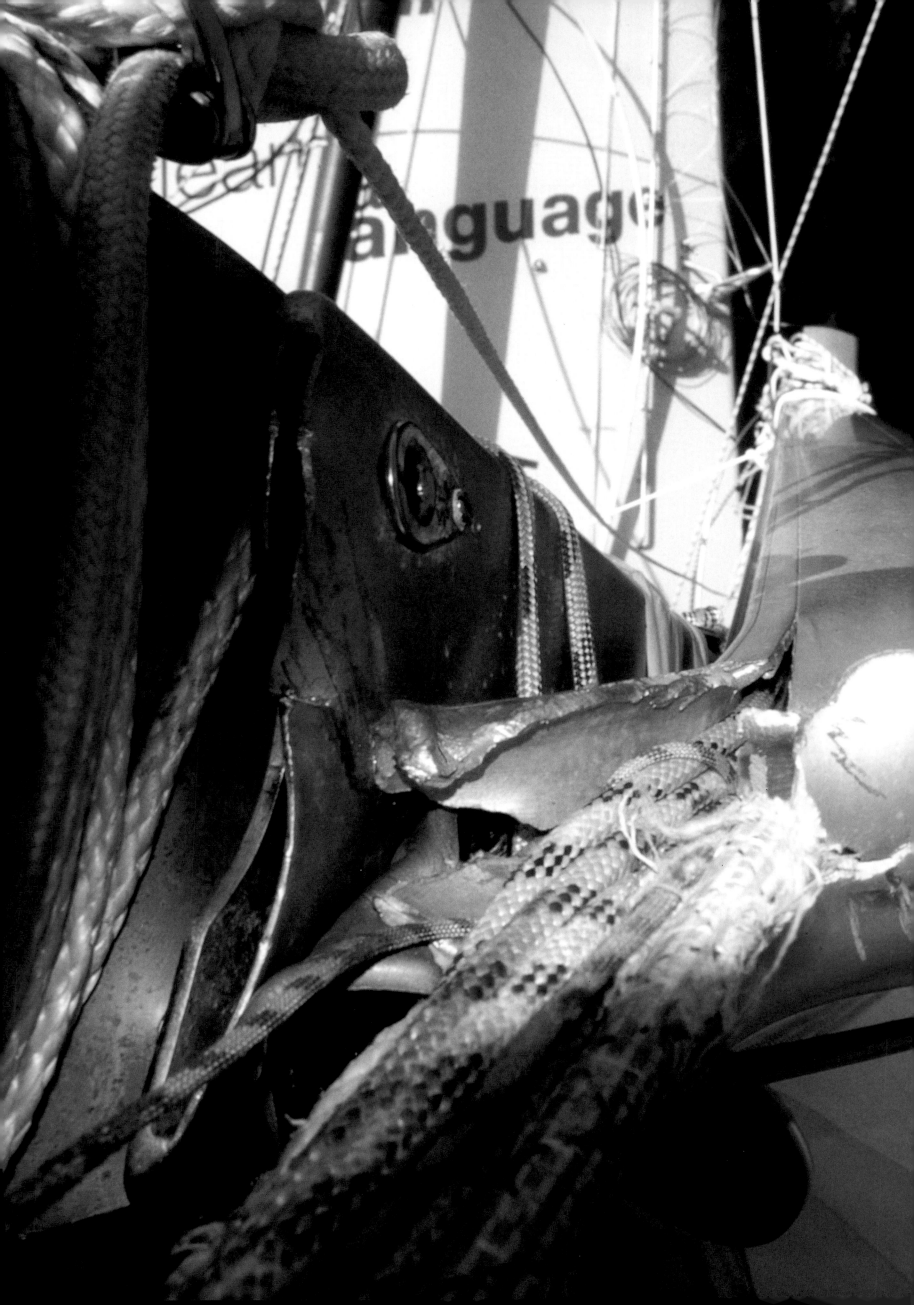

THE MAST ARRIVES IN A CHARTERED ARGENTINE HERCULES.

THE BROKEN MAST IS LIFTED ASHORE IN USHUAIA.

NEXT PAGE: EF EDUCATION PATIENTLY AWAITS HER NEW MAST AT THE DOCK IN USHUAIA.

THE CROWN PASSES

131

While the crew aboard EF Education struggled to Ushuaia, the rest of the fleet was hammering eastwards. The tiny rogue low that came through first gave way to a succession of larger depressions. Everyone experienced the kind of heavy air downwind conditions for which the Southern Ocean is renowned. With boats sailing side by side there was no incentive to back off. Silk Cut paid the penalty when her rig crashed down – and her Southern Ocean crown lay there for the taking. And as the schedules turned into days, and one relentless day after another turned into a week, two boats were slowly creeping away from the fleet. By midday GMT on Day Twelve, EF Language led Swedish Match by twenty-five nautical miles, with the next boat, Merit Cup, another sixty nautical miles behind.

Magnus:

By this stage, the contrast to our Leg Two experience was so dramatic that it was hard to believe that that desperate struggle had ever occurred. We had taken the lead in exactly the same hard-running conditions that we had failed in previously. But while our best run had been only a mile and a half short of Silk Cut's twenty-four-hour record, we hadn't done anything particularly special. We had taken a mile here, a mile there but – most importantly – we had never gone backwards. This didn't just happen, we made changes throughout the boat, and they all had a positive impact. There were some simple things – like the heater. On the second leg this had worked erratically at best, and it had been bitterly cold as a consequence. Kimo had suffered the first stages of frostbite in several fingers and had to have special treatment on his hands in Fremantle. But on Leg Five, Klabbe worked the miracle and kept it running constantly. The difference was enormous – clothes were

still damp, but they were warm to put on. Often, the hardest thing to do in the Southern Ocean is just to get out of your bunk. And your feelings about getting up are crucial to setting your mood for the watch to come. Putting on warm clothes is a big step in the right direction.

The second change was that Paul concentrated more on sailing the boat. He left such strategic concerns as there were to Rudi. And he shifted his focus almost entirely to the night-time. Sailing the Southern Ocean is difficult enough in daylight. But in complete darkness, it's rare to see the moon through the clouds, the waves and the squalls arrive without any visual warning. On Leg Two, all our grimmest moments were at night. Having the extra driver on deck then meant we all spent less time helming. That keeps you sharper when you are at the wheel. And having Paul more aware of the conditions – when the need to be fast and safe was greatest – put him in a better position to make the difficult decisions about sail changes.

We also sailed the boat differently. We learnt that when she started to feel the slightest bit skittish with a fractional spinnaker up, taking a reef in the mainsail balanced the boat and made it more controllable. It was no slower, because you could sail a little higher much more safely. But the biggest change was that we moved everything that wasn't screwed down as far

back in the boat as it would go. The food was stored behind the bulkhead just in front of the rudder post. All the other movable equipment was jammed back against it. While the toilet was being used, or the cooking was being done, no one else was allowed forward. Everyone ate while they were crowded around Rudi's navigation pod, which is all the way back aft under the wheels. People were even sleeping to leeward, which is normally unheard of, because getting the weight aft was more important than keeping it to windward. The same thing applied on deck. The sail stack was taken off the windward rail and shifted to the very back of the boat, right up against the push-pit rails. There it was piled several feet high with every sail we could safely tie down. And finally, the whole watch came aft behind the helmsman with the exception of the spinnaker (and occasionally the mainsail) grinder.

The total weight transfer was perhaps a ton of gear and people, moved back about two metres. If we had trimmed the boat like that in the dock, the bow would have been sticking out of the water at a crazy angle. But it made an unbelievable difference in those heavy-air running conditions. Weight in the back of the boat kept her from nose-diving, and the rudder gripped to the water. You could feel the difference on the wheel. The boat wasn´t so skittish, giving more prior warning before it took control from you. The same sails

PAUL CAYARD.

could be carried for the same wind speeds – but with a much greater safety factor.

And the final change was that we were more conservative. The helmsman was the arbiter on the sail area, and when he was unhappy the sail came down. Similarly, we held off longer before changing to a bigger sail when the breeze seemed to be easing. And always the wind went right back up. Perhaps we had been lucky, but it had worked. We had not had any bad crashes, broaches or broken gear, and had suffered no major downtime. We had broken the A6 and the A5.5, but not seriously. And both had been repaired quickly by Marco, without a backlog being created, without much disruption to the routine. The schedules had clicked by, and even when we thought we had been too conservative and slow, at worse we were pacing the fleet. Everything we were doing was working. We just had to keep doing it – or did we?

Swedish Match was still with us. Still only twenty-five nautical miles behind and dangerously positioned to the south, where we felt the advantage would be on the run-in to Cape Horn. We needed a little extra something to break her grip. Could we afford to push a little harder now? Had we learnt enough? Or should we settle for the distance we already had? Rudi believed that the leader at Cape Horn would gain even more as they turned up the coast. High pressure was threatening from the north-west, and it could turn a

reasonable lead into an unassailable one if it trapped everyone else in light air. If there was ever a time to go for it, this was it.

All these thoughts were in my head as I struggled on deck that day for the 14.00 watch change, when Stevie and I would take over from Crusty and Kimo. They had had the masthead spinnaker up for a couple of hours, the A6 – the big Kahuna as we call it. It's always good to be on deck a little early when you take over the wheel in heavy air. It gives you time to get in tune with the conditions. I could see that the wind had built a little since they had changed up to this sail from the fractional A7 spinnaker. But the waves were perfect, a long, rolling swell lined up with the wind direction and making it easier rather than harder to sail the boat. It was a stunning day, blowing about twenty-five knots, rare spears of sunlight breaking through the cloud cover. The guys were happy with the sail, happy with the conditions. But just as happy to get below and get some rest and some food. It was our turn.

The first few minutes are the most anxious – you forget you were doing the job quite happily just a few hours earlier. But you quickly get your touch back, and it wasn't long before I realised that today was special. Perhaps it was the sun, lighting up the foam and spray. Perhaps it was just the mood on board. Everyone was happy, totally into their job. Perhaps it

134

EVERYTHING THAT COULD BE MOVED WAS PACKED INTO THE STERN OF THE BOAT.

EVEN IN THE SUPPOSED 'COMFORT' OF HIS NAVIGATION STATION, MARK RUDIGER WEARS GLOVES, BALACLAVA AND
COVERS THE COMPUTER KEYBOARDS WITH PLASTIC.

135

was the boat, comfortable in her new trim, with our new techniques, responding to being treated right. Perhaps it was a combination of all these things ... Whatever, the feeling was there.

I rarely saw the speedo dip under twenty knots, and it was surging much faster as we went down the waves. The amount of water rolling along the deck was much less than it had been in the second leg, because of all the weight aft. The boat slowed less into the back of each wave, and I had a lot more control. For the first couple of hours we just charged quite happily through the Southern Ocean, and then it was Stevie's turn. But the breeze was slowly building, pushing up to thirty knots. That was the limit for this sail. Still, we felt good, we felt under control - but what about the mast? With the women and Silk Cut struggling home with jury rigs, I was very conscious of the risk – especially as I was responsible for the mast. I stuck my head down to the navigator's hatch and yelled at Rudi to see if Paul was around.

There were a couple of minutes while Rudi went and found him, then: 'What's up, Magnus?'

I bent back down to the hatch, peering into the gloom below. 'I'm a little concerned for the mast, it's blowing very hard up here, seeing steady thirty now.'

'How does it feel? Does she feel safe?'

'The sailing is fine, but the loads must be very close to maximum.'

There was a silence. I let him think.

'Magnus, if you and Stevie feel happy on the wheel,

and you're not going to crash it, then I'd like to keep it going. I think the big loads are when we crash.'

I was silent now, but I already knew the answer: the sailing felt good. 'I think we are happy.'

'OK, then press on, send her, Magnus.'

I sat back on the couch – the big sail stack aft – before getting back up and checking the safety strops on the backstays. Then I looked over the boat. Nothing was unusual, nothing was out of place. I mentally worked my way through the crucial topmast backstay system that was holding the mast in the boat, starting at the Spinlock jammer on the floor, and following through to the blocks and line of the purchase system, the Sparcraft snap-shackles which held that to the Kevlar backstay, the PBO strop into the mast and finally the end fitting. I thought about all the loads and tried to figure out what would break first. And I decided that it would be the spinnaker. For the first time in my life I was glad that we had already broken a sail. Because however well Marco had repaired it down below on that small sewing machine, it couldn't possibly be as strong as it was before. That thought reassured me, I sat back, and took up the mainsheet again.

It was probably about 17.30 when Paul emerged out of the hatch. It was about three hours before darkness, and I was back on the wheel. By then we were just hurling the boat through the ocean. Over waves, through them, the boat just kept motoring. Nothing slowed her, nothing stopped her stride, there was so

A CHILEAN NAVY PLANE RECORDS EF LANGUAGE, FIRST TO ROUND CAPE HORN (ABOVE AND OPPOSITE).

much power from the rig. How does it go – power is nothing without control? But we had control, the rudder had grip. And I had the boat, I knew she was happy. Even so, perhaps feeling that this ride could not go on for ever, I had reached the point where I would be willing to change down. Paul joined the guys on the couch, sat quietly and watched for a while. Then he was beside me, yelling in my ear to be heard through all the clothing: 'How does it feel, Magnus?'

'Pretty good actually,' I shouted back, hesitating for a moment to give the wheel a big spin. 'There's a lot of wind, but she feels fine.'

'OK Magnus, let's roll with it, I'm happy.'

Then he moved forward and swopped on to the grinder. Now, when someone like Paul Cayard is grinding, you kind of know that the trimming is going to be right on the money. It gives you confidence. I needed it; by now it was blowing up to thirty-five knots. We had struggled on previous occasions to hold that sail in anything above thirty knots. It was an incredible feeling to be at the wheel of this charging machine. She simply didn't hesitate, carving a trough through the Southern Ocean, hurling solid walls of spray into the sunshine. We were sailing down a tunnel of water and light. A sensory overload, trying to pound through the bridge of concentration

I had built up for the conditions. Filtering out the feedback I needed from the waves, the wind and the boat. Trying to stem the wild rushes of sound and motion, damp down the adrenaline-soaked excitement. And there was Paul, winding like crazy, giving me these huge grins when we clocked it over thirty knots, with the boys on the couch behind whooping and hollering. They were moments I will never forget.

There are many special times in the Whitbread. The Southern Ocean is always special – one way or another. So is rounding Cape Horn. And of course winning is special too – that, after all, is what you are there for. As it turned out, on this leg we would do all these things. But sometimes it is the pure experience that is the best. Knowing you have reached down and found the ability in yourselves, together, as a team, to do something that seemed utterly impossible only a few short weeks before. Smoking through the Southern Ocean, the big Kahuna up, and thirty-five knots on both the wind-speed and boat-speed dials.

Our watch ended at 20.00, about half an hour before sunset. We held that sail right through to the end. The extra hands coming up made it the perfect time to change, just before darkness. I'm sure that was what Paul had planned all along. It was still a difficult change, fully powered up, going like crazy. But the contrast to the disastrous affair on Leg Two could not have been more marked. We were changing to the A7 in almost the same conditions as we had on the second leg, when we had come so close to hurting Curtis badly. But instead of it being a forced change to a bigger sail after breaking the right one, this was a comfortable change down, after a day in which it would have been hard to imagine the boat could be sailed any faster. And with the masthead down and the fractional up, the boat felt very good as darkness fell. There was a feeling of real relief that we had done our pushing and now was the time to back off the throttle and see what the results were.

The schedule came in a couple of hours after I went below: our lead had grown to just under fifty nautical miles. Better still, Swedish Match had come north, and was now only a handful of miles south of our line through the Southern Ocean. The push had been worth it, we hadn't crashed, and we'd got the jump we needed. This time we had stayed right on that fine line. It was the best performance possible. Perhaps we had been a little more fortunate, but we had learnt our lessons, and applied them well. You can never control the Southern Ocean, but you can ride with it.

The fifty nautical mile lead had turned in to eighty nautical miles by the end of the next twenty-four hours. EF Language rounded Cape Horn first on February 15 at 11.15. It was a stunning victory, all the more so for the incredible turn-around after Leg Two – it was clear on whose heads Silk Cut's crown now lay. And as EF Language turned north up the

coast of Argentina, high pressure was already dropping like a blanket on the rest of the fleet. EF Language escaped the light air and powered on to the finish. The lead at Cape Horn turned into a winning margin of more than three days and three hours. Behind her the leading pack of Swedish Match, Merit Cup, Toshiba and Innovation Kvaerner got badly trapped by high pressure a second time, after finally rounding Cape Horn.

Behind them Chessie Racing had briefly stopped just north of Cape Horn to pick up spares for her generator. But being behind turned out to be an advantage. They set off again just as the high pressure ridge lifted to the west, and by staying a little further east moved into third place. BrunelSunergy also arrived with the new breeze, but went east of the Falklands, to go around everyone and into second place. It was BrunelSunergy's best finish so far. For Team EF it was a mixed blessing. It helped to put the group chasing EF Language for overall honours a few more points behind. Her lead over Merit Cup going into Leg Six was ninety-six points. But it put BrunelSunergy a jump ahead of the women. After the broken rig they found themselves in last place overall for the first time. But worse was to follow for Toshiba. She was disqualified from Leg Five during the stopover for failing to properly report the use of her engine to clear weed. As a consequence Toshiba scored zero points for the leg. Only six boats had correctly completed the toughest section of the race.

OAKLEY MASKS WERE ESSENTIAL IN BLAST-REACHING CONDITIONS, BECAUSE OF THE PHENOMENAL VOLUME OF WATER OVER THE DECK.

NEXT PAGE: STEVE ERICKSON AND JOSH BELSKY RELAX ON THE 'COUCH' – WHILE TRIMMING IN FORTY KNOTS OF BREEZE.

EF LANGUAGE'S TRIUMPHANT ARRIVAL IN SÃO SEBASTIÃO WAS IN THE MIDDLE OF THE NIGHT
– AND IN THE MIDDLE OF CARNIVAL – NEITHER DETERRED THE PRESS.
PREVIOUS PAGE: THE CREW OF EF LANGUAGE CELEBRATE THEIR ROUNDING OF THE 'CORN' – CAPE HORN.
THE CROWN IS PASSED – MAGNUS OLSSON HOLDS THE ROARING FORTIES
TROPHY FOR THE BEST SOUTHERN OCEAN PERFORMANCE.

ANOTHER DAY AT THE OFFICE

Leg Six – 4,750 nautical miles from São Sebastião to Fort Lauderdale - started quietly, with the fleet crawling across the line amidst a vast and chaotic spectator fleet. Then a small but intense low-pressure system developed right over São Sebastião and hurled the boats across Rio Bay. The trough it left behind as it died caused some difficult squally conditions, but progress up the coast remained fast, thanks to the trade winds. The high-pressure systems in both the South and North Atlantic were building strongly, compressing the Doldrums, as everyone placed their bets for the crossing. Toshiba was leading and chose west, with EF Education on her line but some twenty nautical miles behind. EF Language was in the middle pack, while Merit Cup and Swedish Match were out on the eastern flank. The east looked good as the western boats fought their way through more difficult conditions. As the fleet broke clear of the Doldrums and back into settled trade wind conditions, the women found themselves once more trailing the fleet.

Anna:

The hand on my shoulder was light. I turned quickly and looked up, eyes open but unseeing. 'Ten minutes,' said the voice. I stared at the underside of the deck above me until the world came into focus. A trickle of condensation rolled off a screwhead and slid down the hull until it disappeared. The silk sheet was twisted around me, damp with sweat. I rolled clear of it and slid off the bunk. The boat's motion was easy, the sea flat. I fumbled in my bag for the still-damp shorts and T-shirt. Leah, who came on watch with me, was just stirring from the other top windward bunk. Dressed, I found a water bottle and filled it, before climbing up through the hatch and peering into the soft light of dawn. I flipped my sunglasses off my forehead and into place – it was bright enough to need them. And it was still blisteringly hot, which was no surprise when you consider that the water temperature had only just dropped below thirty degrees.

Katie glanced across at me from the leeward trimming position and mumbled, 'Hello.' She didn't have sunglasses on and I could see her eyes were bloodshot, tired from the night watch, from the strain of peering at the sail in the dark, trying to pick up the shape and movement of the telltales with the torch.

I struggled out of the hatch, moved down to leeward and stuck my full water bottle in the forward tail bag. 'Anybody seen the sunblock?' I asked of no one in particular, and no one replied. I checked the two leeward bags: ropes, a soggy power bar wrapper, two empty water bottles and a torch that didn't work, but no sunblock. I moved up to windward and checked in both those bags, and there was nothing there either. 'Anybody seen the sunblock?' I said again, a little more insistently, moving aft as I checked around the faces.

Melissa glanced away from the mainsail leech telltale. 'We haven't touched it.'

I stuck my head into the bag on the leeward side of the mainsheet grinder.

'It's been dark,' said someone, with more than a trace of sarcasm.

But I didn't care, I'd found it. I held the bottle up triumphantly to the group, and pulled a face. They all smiled. I moved up to the windward side and sat on the sail stack while I smothered myself. Then I went through my short, tropical sailing check list: water bottle, sunglasses, sunblock. I was ready. I checked my watch: just before six. I slid forward again and sat beside Katie.

'So what's happening, Katie?'

She looked back at me, turning from the headsail. 'The wind eased back a little about three hours ago, and moved right a touch, so we went with this.'

I glanced up at the A3.

Katie was still talking. 'We set up for a spinnaker, in case the wind kept going. But it's been pretty stable ever since, just rolling us up the track, nice and easy.'

I nodded and cast my eye critically over the huge sail. The so-called Monstas, Code Zeros or Whompers had caused a lot of fuss early on. Team EF had been the first to develop the sail, and the crew on Language had used them to particularly impressive effect on the first leg. The other skippers had stirred up trouble in Cape Town, but the race officials had confirmed again that they were legal, and the rest of the fleet had been playing catch-up in sail development ever since. The controversy centred on the fact that although the sail measured in as a spinnaker, it could be used at wind angles that were normally the territory of headsails. Because spinnakers could be raised to the masthead, rather than just the hounds, the A3 had an enormous amount of extra sail area compared to a conventional headsail, and in light to moderate breeze, that translated directly into speed.

'I was thinking maybe I should ease the guy a touch,' said Katie.

'I was wondering about that too.' I scrambled aft to where the leeward after-guy was made up on the runner winch drum. The A3 was hoisted on the masthead spinnaker halyard, and fastened to the downhaul at the bow. It was furled when we set it and dropped it, because the sail was impossible to hoist loose. Once it was up, we controlled the sail by using the leeward spinnaker sheet run on to the primary winch drum, as well as the leeward after-guy. The turning blocks for both sheets were on the gunwale, but the after-guy lead was much further forward and allowed us to put tension almost directly down the leech. The spinnaker sheet tensioned the foot. By juggling these two sheets, you could get the sail shape you wanted.

'You happy?' said Katie as I sat back beside her, adjustment completed.

'Definitely,' I replied. She handed me the sheet and I slid into her place by the winch. Katie was gone in a moment, then Kiny brushed past me as she followed her below. I glanced aft: Melissa now had the wheel; she would go down at eight, along with Bridget and Keryn. Leah sat with Melissa on the high side, getting a feel for the conditions in the same way that I had with Katie. I popped in some chewing gum, and eased the sheet a fraction, Keryn cracked the mainsheet off behind me. The A3 is so big that the mainsail has to be trimmed around it – if we eased the leech of the A3 then we had to ease the mainsail leech to maintain the parallel slot. The windspeed jumped up to thirteen knots, the wind angle steady around 110 degrees. The first morning watch change was complete.

'Whoa, dolphins!' shouted Leah a couple of minutes later. I turned round to see her already bounding off the deck towards the companionway. I knew where she was going – Leah was responsible for all the video and still photography shot on board. We had seen an extraordinary amount of wildlife, and with Lynnath being a marine biologist, I'm sure we'd also learnt a great deal more about it than the other crews. But no matter what amazing creatures we saw, Leah could never resist the chance for some dolphin photos!

It was seven-thirty when Bridget slid past me to get breakfast started, and fifteen minutes later nothing else had changed. I hadn't touched the sheet or guy. In those circumstances we can afford a couple of people below, and I slid down for a breakfast of cereal with some freeze-dried fruit. There was no coffee. With only two days to turn the boat around in São Sebastião, somehow the coffee had got left behind. Maybe that wasn't such a bad thing, we saved a lot of gas by not having hot drinks. But it wasn't the only thing we were missing. The minimal rest had left everybody jaded. It hadn't been a problem until we had hit the demanding, try-the-patience-of-a-saint conditions of the Doldrums. Perhaps our concentration wasn't there, or maybe we had just been unlucky; either way, we got nailed by more bad clouds than anyone else. We had fallen off the back of the fleet, and had been reaching ever since, with little opportunity to catch up, and none to overtake. Sometimes sailing could be a brutal sport.

When I had finished breakfast, I swopped with Leah at the wheel, and she ate with the three coming up. I watched Bridget, Keryn and Melissa go below with more than a little envy. Still, I was steering now,

151

REACHING IN STABLE TRADE WIND CONDITIONS IS ABOUT THE MOST PLEASANT SAILING ANYWHERE – BUT LEAVES LITTLE IN THE WAY OF OPPORTUNITY FOR CATCHING OR OVERTAKING THE OPPOSITION.

which made a change from staring at the headsail. When Leah returned she took over the trimming. Marleen was on the mainsheet, Lisa grinding for her and Joan sat on the gunwale, near me.

'Puff coming,' she would warn occasionally, and would bear away just a fraction. The big sail loaded up frighteningly quickly. But she had been staring out at the horizon silently for a while, when she asked, 'What day is it?'

'Huh?' I glanced at her.

'What day is it?'

I looked back at the boat-speed read-out: I hadn't lost anything through that glance away. 'I've no idea,' I said finally. 'Maybe Tuesday or Wednesday, why?'

'No reason. I just wondered. Have you got any gum?'

I fumbled in my pockets and handed her a piece. Then she lapsed into silence again, until Lisa tapped her on the shoulder to swop onto the mainsheet grinder. Not that there was a lot of grinding to do, the wind was relentlessly steady. The boat was beautifully balanced, fully powered up, water tanks full, sails stacked, and with the sea flat and a cloudless sky, it was perfect sailing weather.

'You know,' said Lisa, now sitting beside me, 'I think the wind might be getting up a little. I was thinking I might set the sheets up for the reacher. In case we have to change.'

I looked at her doubtfully. 'I haven't really noticed it myself, she still feels pretty comfortable to me.'

'Yeah, but just in case.'

'OK.' It was, after all, something to do.

Lisa peeled off the rail and moved forward. The job didn't take her long. But an hour later the wind, if anything, was easing a little and moving aft, to the right. 'I think it would be the spinnaker next,' I said to Leah.

She looked back at me, then at the instruments, then back to Lisa on the handles. 'You want to set it up?'

Lisa nodded and Joan dropped off the rail to take her place. Inevitably, ten minutes later the wind had gone back to where it was before. I swopped with Leah, and went back to the headsail trim.

I glanced at my watch. Two hours to go before we were relieved. I turned back to the others. 'Shouldn't there have been a sched about now?'

Leah was at the wheel, and didn't take her eyes off the headsail when she replied, 'Probably.' She hesitated; I watched her gaze shift to the instruments on the mast, and then back to the headsail again. 'Do you really want to know?'

I looked back at the telltales myself. The windward bottom ribbon was lifting slightly, so I wound the sheet on a touch and it came back into line. I heard the mainsheet grind round the drum behind me in sympathy. The boat-speed flickered up a tenth of a knot. Finally I looked back at Leah and sighed. 'Probably not,' I said.

The last hour crawled by. It was Katie appearing out of the hatch that told me the watch was finally done. She stepped on to the deck and stretched. She peered slowly around the horizon, before alighting on the Code 0. 'Same sail,' she said, more statement than question.

'Uhuh,' I replied.

She peered up at the trim, then rested her gaze on the instrument dials. 'Same course.' Another statement.

'That too,' I answered.

'And certainly no new boats to see. What about the wind?'

'It went up a bit, went down a bit, pretty much the same.'

There was a silence, while she once more scanned the horizon, all blue sparkling ocean and puffy white clouds. 'Beautiful day though.'

I looked up and smiled at her. 'Just another day at the office.'

The reaching conditions were maintained almost to the finish. The wind conspired to stretch the fleet, providing better direction and speed for the boats ahead. There were no more passing lanes and the women once again had to accept last place. They arrived in Fort Lauderdale only a handful of hours off the pace, but a world away from those precious extra points. Most of the crew had been at sea for all but two days of the past two months, and sailed and raced over ten thousand miles.

The men aboard EF Language had come out of the Doldrums in second place. Although they took the lead from Silk Cut for a while, they lost it again off Barbuda, and from there the fleet had extended. But both the closest boats overall were behind them – Swedish Match in third and Merit Cup in fifth – and once again their overall points lead increased. Innovation Kvaerner split these two in fourth, while Chessie Racing and Toshiba came in sixth and seventh, with the Dutch aboard BrunelSunergy in eighth. Apart from some broken sails on the first night there was little damage, but Fort Lauderdale allowed the fleet to recuperate from the effects of days of broiling weather and damp conditions, while the impressive marine facilities permitted everyone to complete a full maintenance programme. During this respite EF Language changed to a new mast. They were taking no chances.

153

BOWMEN MUSTN'T SUFFER FROM A FEAR OF HEIGHTS, AFTER EVERY SPINNAKER HOIST THEY HAVE TO GO TO THE MASTHEAD TO ATTACH
THE HALYARD STROP, AND SPINNAKER CHANGES OFTEN REQUIRE A TRIP TO THE END OF THE POLE.
NEXT PAGE: MARLEEN CLEYNDERT DRINKS A VITAMIN SUPPLEMENT BEFORE GOING ON DECK FOR HER WATCH.

BETWEEN THE NORTHERN AND SOUTHERN HEMISPHERE TRADE WINDS LIE THE DOLDRUMS – LIGHT AIR MIXED WITH SQUALLS
AND HEAVY RAIN SHOWERS. DIFFICULT SAILING – BUT SPICED BY THE POTENTIAL FOR MAJOR GAINS AND LOSSES.

BRIDGET SUCKLING (LEFT).

NEXT PAGE: DRIFTER UP, SO IT'S WEIGHT FORWARD AND TO LEEWARD, EVEN WHILE MAINTAINING THE RUNNING RIGGING.

THE WEATHER BRIEFING

The seventh leg – an 870-nautical-mile sprint from Fort Lauderdale to Baltimore – started when the gun went on April 19. But the sailing is so inextricably mixed with the preparation that this leg, like all the others, started in the minds of the sailors several days before, when they got their first look at the weather forecast. While the shore crew and the rest of the sailing team prepared the boat, the skippers, navigators and watch captains of EF Language and Education spent a couple of hours a day considering what lay before them.

Magnus:

I rocked the chair onto its
two rear legs and leant back, staring at the familiar ceiling. We had had so many of these rooms – containers and mobile trailers – in the stop-over ports. They were all different and yet somehow all the same: the cheap plastic, metal and Formica furniture; the tiled floors and ceiling; the imitation wood veneer; the same clutter of EF bags and jackets, charts and computers, weather maps and memos. I let the chair fall forward and said, 'So, Clouds, are we ready to start?' Roger 'Clouds' Badham looked up from the computer in front of him. 'If everyone's here.' There was a murmur of agreement from around the room. Getting everyone together for these meetings wasn't easy; you had to get going before someone drifted back out of the door again. Clouds handed out the sets of information he had printed and copied for us. That was the thing about Clouds, wherever we were in the world, he was always extremely well prepared.

166

Combined with an open approach and vast experience, it made him one of the most sought-after meteorologists in sailing. We were lucky to have him for the duration of the race. He started, 'This is today's forecast, and you'll see that the general situation has not changed that much. The cold front is still lying over to the north-north-west of the race track, from Georgia across the Carolinas. And it's still forecast to roll south-east out into the Atlantic, early Monday morning local time. If anything, the latest forecasts have moved it forward a touch.' There was a rustling of paper as everyone flipped through the charts. 'At the moment we have pretty much a southerly breeze ahead of the cold front, blowing at fifteen to eighteen knots. Under the cloud – the front itself – there is probably going to be some light rain and softer breeze. I'll update this just before the start tomorrow, but you should get a quick windshift in this lighter air, from the south-west to north-west. From there it will build in strength again, and continue to shift more slowly through the north and into the north-east.' Clouds looked up at the group, and there was a few moments' silence while everyone digested this information.

'So, Clouds, how does that affect what we talked about yesterday, going east and cutting the corner?' asked Paul finally.

'The choice is still there. You can follow the Gulf Stream north of the start line, and go with it as it swings in a bend north-east towards Cape Hatteras. At the moment ...' Clouds paused while he turned the computer round, and brought up a colour satellite photograph of the south-east coast of the USA, 'the Gulf Stream's sitting about six miles off the coast here at Lauderdale, although we've seen it as close as two or three miles, and as far out as eight miles. Once you're in it the most favourable current is on the western edge, anything up to four knots, maybe more in places. Going with the Gulf Stream adds about..., what did we say yesterday, Rudi?'

'Thirty-five miles,' replied Rudi.

'Adds thirty-five miles to the course compared to the eastern route, the straight line to Cape Hatteras which cuts the corner on the bend in the Gulf Stream. So you only need one extra knot of current for the day and a half and you'll be in the stream to make that thirty-five miles up. It should be easy to do.'

'But what about the front?' said Paul.

'The eastern route is better for the cold front. And the slower the front moves, the better the eastern route gets. Because the longer you're ahead of the front, the longer you have stronger southerly, pre-frontal winds. But if the front moves quickly, then the advantage will be short-lived. So you can't be confident about the benefits of going east, it depends on the unpredictable speed of the cold front.'

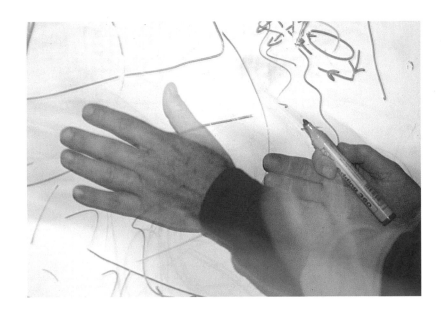

ROGER BADHAM EXPLAINS HIS FORECAST.

'So it's possible it could work, but risky?' That was Paul again.

'You can be sure the Gulf Stream will be there if you go the western route,' chipped in Rudi.

'That's right.' concurred Clouds. 'It's my judgement that the eastern route is too risky. You will definitely get the assistance of the Gulf Stream if you go west, you may not get help from the cold front if you go east.'

'Maybe we have to particularly consider the situation we're in now,' added Paul. 'This isn't the first leg any more. We have a hundred and fifteen point lead, we have to pay attention to where Swedish Match and Merit Cup are going to go.'

There was a silence. Clouds was just about to start speaking again, when a low background hum gathered intensity into an ear-splitting roar. We were right under the flight path to Fort Lauderdale airport, and these conversation breaks were a regular part of life. As the noise of the aero engine dimmed Clouds took up his line of thought again. 'It's possible that Swedish Match could go for it, they've played the edges of the course a lot so far.'

'They only just got away with it last time though. They don't want to go back behind Merit Cup.' Kimo was referring to the eastern route Swedish Match had taken up the coast of Brazil. Over fifty miles behind at one point, they had only just recovered to a third place when the eastern exit from the Doldrums had paid off.

'I still think if anybody is going that way it would be BrunelSunergy, they have nothing to lose. Maybe

Silk Cut too; Lawrie really needs those big scores to save his regatta. Same with Toshiba,' I added. 'They both took more chances on the last leg than previously. They could go for it again.'

'It's such a short leg, though, people will be nervous of a loss that they have no time to recover,' said Stevie.

'If it's anyone, I'd say it'll be BrunelSunergy. And we can only take that risk if Swedish Match does,' said Paul, with an air of finality.

The talk went on for another couple of hours, with more details of points and tactics, cold eddies and eastern walls, and arrival prospects for the Chesapeake Bay. Curt, Stevie, Rudi and Paul had spent a total of eighteen days in the Chesapeake Bay between them. They had a lot to report and discuss, checking the local wind effects with Clouds. Some of it was ground we had covered earlier in the week, some of it we would cover again tomorrow. But that was the idea, the more you thought about the different possible scenarios in advance and reached an agreed conclusion, the faster you could react out on the water. The meeting broke up just before eleven, and we all returned to our separate schedules.

Leg Seven started in glorious sunshine and the fast downwind conditions that Clouds had forecast. If anything it was a little windier, and the fleet screamed through the buoys off Fort Lauderdale and out into the Gulf Stream. Everyone set up on starboard gybe and headed north-north-east in the southerly breeze. But the fleet was slowly crossing the stream, all approaching the eastern edge, still

FROM THE TOP; BOAT-SPEED, WINDSPEED, TRUE WIND ANGLE, APPARENT WIND ANGLE AND COMPASS HEADING.

on starboard gybe. The moment when the choice they had discussed, to carry on and cut the corner or gybe back to port, into the favourable current, was fast approaching.

We were using the 'inshore' or 'full-court-press' watch system that we used to finish legs, and that had proved so effective going into Sydney. Three watches of three men, with two watches on deck at once, plus either Paul or Curt. It was fantastic sailing, the masthead 0.75-ounce spinnaker was up and the boat topping twenty knots for long periods. The sky was filled with stars; moonless, warm, quite beautiful. It was about two in the morning local time, with Rudi on radar watch and Paul getting some rest. Curt was on the mainsheet with Stevie steering, Marco had the spinnaker sheet and Klabbe was grinding for him. I sat on the weather rail with Juggy and Curtis, watching the opposition and anything else that mattered, like the wind direction. 'We have a little windshift,' I said to Curt. 'The port gybe would be just as close to the course now.'

Curt glanced over his shoulder. 'I was just thinking that. Swedish's still going, is she?'

'Yeah, maybe a couple of miles back. She's just to windward of our line, I can see her red light.'

Rudi stuck his head through the navigation hatch.

'Keep your eyes on those guys, we're starting to drop out of the current a little, and I think Kvaerner's already gybed.'

'You think Swedish will go back to the Gulf Stream, Rudi?' I asked him before he disappeared.

Rudi looked thoughtful. 'If he doesn't gybe soon, we have to start thinking about the fact that he might not, that he might go east.'

'Would we go out there with him?'

'I kind of think we should stick with him, like we said before,' said Curt, 'Unless it's a really stupid option going east, then maybe not. We have to think about Merit Cup too.'

'It's not stupid, it is a real option, just riskier because you're relying on the cold front for the gains rather than the Gulf Stream,' said Rudi. We all knew the arguments off by heart now and there was a silence amongst those aft, broken only by the pounding of the forward winches as Marco hauled us on to a wave with a massive trim of the sheet.

'I think I'll just look at it all again,' said Rudi, finally.

He had only got halfway down the hatch when Juggy interrupted the resumed silence. 'She's gybed,' he said sharply. 'At least I think she has ... Yes! I can see a green light now. I'm sure Swedish has gybed.'

'I'll check the bearing,' I said and brought up the

hand-bearing compass. Rudi had already gone below. I peered across the wildly swinging luminous numbers, trying to catch them steady for a moment, get a feel for the dance, find the pattern so I could take a reasonable average. Not easy when you're rolling downwind at twenty knots and the target is over two miles away. But finally I was happy with the trend. 'He's gaining bearing, I think Juggy's right.'

'Rudi?' yelled Curt down the hatch.

'We now have two targets gaining bearing on the radar. If you're sure one of them's Swedish, I'm happy to gybe.'

'It's a no-brainer then, set it up,' said Curt, 'No rush, plenty of time, let's do a nice job.'

Unknown to the crew of EF Language at the time, BrunelSunergy had already taken the decision to cut the corner and go the eastern, direct route. They had done so in a meeting, just like Team EF's, the previous day. And although they were the only boat to continue on starboard, the strategy worked. The front co-operated, slowing over the rest of the fleet, and then speeding up to cross BrunelSunergy. When she rejoined the other eight boats off Cape Hatteras, BrunelSunergy had a thirty-mile advantage.

Despite that, onboard EF Language they were happy. They had stayed close to Swedish Match as both boats played the western side of the course. There they had found better currents than the rest of the fleet and jumped ahead to second and third. Locked together, they ground down their deficit to BrunelSunergy to only five miles at the finish. But this time Swedish Match got the better of EF Language and grabbed second by twenty-eight seconds. Nevertheless, EF Language would go into Leg Eight needing only to finish within one place of Swedish Match to win the Whitbread. Marco Constant, however, would miss the leg, he had broken his right wrist badly in a fall down the companionway just before EF Language left the Gulf Stream. Behind them Innovation Kvaerner led home Silk Cut by a few minutes, then Merit Cup, Toshiba, Chessie Racing and EF Education. Ashore, there was more bad news for the trouble-torn Toshiba team. First, navigator Andrew Cape resigned, then they were penalised two places after a protest incident with EF Education. Toshiba was judged to have crossed too close in front of the women – on the give-way port tack – in the dark on the first night.

MARK RUDIGER CHECKS THE CLOUDS ON THE HORIZON FOR A POSSIBLE WIND SHIFT.

THE FORT LAUDERDALE START.

WITH THE GULF STREAM MAINTAINING TROPICAL TEMPERATURES NEAR FORT LAUDERDALE, IT WAS COOLER TO EAT ON DECK.

BUT ONCE OUT OF THE STREAM ON THE APPROACH TO THE CHESAPEAKE BAY TEMPERATURES DROPPED.

175

EF LANGUAGE POWERS OUT OF FORT LAUDERDALE.

PREVIOUS PAGE: THE PATTERN OF THE KEVLAR WEAVE IN A NORTH 3DL HEADSAIL.

A CLOSE START IN FORT LAUDERDALE (LEFT) AND AN EQUALLY CLOSE FINISH IN BALTIMORE (RIGHT).

NEXT PAGE: EF LANGUAGE AGAINST THE BACKDROP OF DOWNTOWN BALTIMORE.

SAIL PHOTOGRAPHS ARE ESSENTIAL TO SAIL DEVELOPMENT.

Leg Eight: a 3,390-nautical-mile transatlantic crossing that started from Annapolis in the Chesapeake Bay and finished in La Rochelle. Once out of the tricky confines of the Bay and into the open ocean, the fleet sailed east towards the favourable current of the Gulf Stream. The boats only left the stream to dash north and squeeze around the top of a south-going high pressure. In doing so they found themselves jammed against the southern edge of the Prohibited Zone, set by the race committee to keep them out of the icebergs flowing south in the Labrador Current. But there was still less than forty miles between the first seven boats as they cleared the Prohibited Zone, with Language in third and Education in fifth. They continued east, chased by a cold front, with its strong south-west and westerly breeze. EF Education had been running hard and fast in twenty to twenty-five knots of wind, when Anna was woken for her watch, just before midday on May 10.

Anna:

I was fumbling around for

my foul-weather trousers, and heaved a pair clear from under the mess of spinnaker that sprawled across the floorboards. It was the A6, a full-size masthead running sail, made from heavy 1.5-ounce cloth. And it was soaking wet, like so much of the boat, in the bitter, damp, grey cold of the North Atlantic. That included the trousers and, unfortunately, once I found the name on the back, I realised that they were mine. I slumped back disconsolately and saw that Katie, who had woken me, was just about to go back on deck. 'Do you want to help me pack this before you go up, Katie?' I said. She turned back from the companionway. 'I'm afraid it needs a bit more than packing. We blew it out an hour or so ago.' I looked at her hesitantly, taking in this information. The two of us would be responsible for fixing it. 'How bad?' I asked cautiously: judging from her expression, I didn't want to know. 'Depends who you talk to.

182

There's a rumour that there's a big hole in it.'

I frowned. 'Very big or just big?'

Katie shrugged. 'We're just going to peel. Once we get that out of the way, we can take a decent look at it. You want to come up and give us a hand?'

I pulled my foul-weather top out from the bunk and followed her on deck. But it was almost four hours before we both got back down together. Keeping enough people on deck through a series of sail changes, the watch change and then lunch, had meant no opportunity even to have a look at the spinnaker. It didn't help that we were right under a cold front and the wind refused to settle. Without the A6 we had a choice of either the A4 or the A5. The A4 was a lighter-cloth, 0.75-ounce full-size running sail, while the A5 was the heavier 1.5-ounce cloth, but a slightly smaller, reaching sail. Of course the wind speed insisted on going up and down right across where the A6 should be used: now a little too light for the smaller reaching spinnaker; then a little too breezy for the lighter cloth of the running sail. Trying to keep the boat going quickly, we peeled seven times that afternoon.

Finally, however, we got the steady north-westerly breeze behind the cold front, and we were able to settle on a reaching headsail and a staysail. Only then, at about four o'clock, did Katie and I get a look at the spinnaker. The A6 was about three hundred square

metres in size. The clear working area at the base of the companionway wasn't even three square metres. We had to shuffle our way through the sail a few metres at a time, finding the damage, making notes, trying to get an idea of what needed to be fixed and how we could do it.

We started by working our way up the edges. It was easy to see that all of the tape that seamed and sealed the leech was off the sail. The tape on the luff had also come off as far as the reinforcement at the top and bottom, about half the length of the luff. After we had worked our way up the edges, we could see that the spinnaker was virtually in two pieces, ripped all the way from the luff to the leech, straight across the sail. If that wasn't bad enough, the rumours about the hole were true. There was a big section missing just behind the luff. I took a deep breath when I saw it, and looked at Katie. Did we have enough cloth?

We carried a lot of fifteen-centimetre-wide strips of spinnaker cloth on the boat, but no large sections. We would have to stick the strips together, and hope that it came to a big enough piece to fill the hole. We laid out the damaged area a section at a time – it was bigger than the work space – and tried to measure it as carefully as we could. Katie and I thought we could just about do it with the material that we had. I went to find Christine. She was in the navigation station with Lynnath and Isabelle, who was the guest crew for this leg. All three looked up as soon as I poked my head round the corner. 'We think we can fix it, but it's a major, it'll take at least two days, and that's with both of us working on it flat out.'

Christine glanced at Isabelle. 'We think you should do it quickly. The forecast says it will be reaching and maybe some light air for a couple of days, then it's going to blow hard from the south-west, and we'll need that sail. You and Katie just work on the spinnaker, don't worry about your watches.'

I nodded. 'OK, we'll get on with it.' I crawled back to Katie and told her the good news. We weren't going to be doing much sleeping for a while.

'No pressure then,' she replied.

We thought the place to start was the rip that separated the top and bottom of the sail. And if we started from the leech and worked our way towards the hole, we could be fairly confident that we were sticking it down in the right shape. Once we had the spinnaker back in one piece, it would be easier to see the form of the missing section. We lay the first few feet of the rip out, then started work. Because the floorboards are a thin layer of resin and fibre sandwiched over foam, it's possible to pin a sail out on to the floorboards, just like you would on the wooden floor of a normal sail loft. Except, of course, that the space is tiny, and it's constantly being used by other people. We had to work on just a couple of feet at a time, pin

it out as neatly as we could, then when the two broken edges were held in place, spray the sail with glue and stick down the spinnaker cloth. We had a glue on board that worked even when the sail was damp – which was fortunate, because the boat wasn't getting any drier. At each of the seven spinnaker changes that afternoon, the A4 and A5 had come down sodden. Condensation now lined the hull, streaming in rivers down the bulkheads.

The one thing that was working in our favour was that the sea was incredibly flat. It was like estuary sailing, the boat hissing along at a good speed, with barely a bump or a murmur. It was then that I really felt for Marco on Language when in the Southern Ocean he'd had three broken spinnakers to fix, one after the other, and all the time the boat screaming along and hurling itself off waves. So it could be worse, I reminded myself every time I looked at the size of the task before us. Yet it seemed impossible when you let yourself think about it . The only way was to take a few feet at a time, keep your head down, get into a routine and work slowly and methodically.

But it was about to get worse. Lisa appeared at my shoulder at the end of her watch and said, 'I guess you'll be expecting to sew that back together again.'

I looked up, something tweaking at my memory. 'Yes ...'

'So you'll be needing the sewing machine?'

183

My heart sank. 'There's a problem with the alternator, isn't there?'

'Sure is, and we've already flattened your sewing machine battery, using it to start the engine to charge the main batteries.'

Katie swore.

'We'll figure it out, fix something up. When will you need the machine?' said Lisa quickly.

'Late tomorrow,' I replied.

'I'll get Keryn to help me. Thank God we're reaching and there's not much to do on deck.'

Lisa headed back to find Keryn. If it could be done, they would work out a way. I went back to warn Christine that it might take a little longer than we had thought – if we could finish the job at all. The forecast hadn't changed, we needed the sail soon.

We kept at it all night, and into the next morning, afternoon and night, working together, each grabbing no more than an hour or so of sleep. After the rip, we unpicked the stitching on the luff tape and stapled it back into place, then reinforced it with more spinnaker tape. Without the watch system to count the hours and days for us, time became a complete blur. The boat's routine served only to irritate and interrupt us. We had to clear the repair out of the way for each wet sail that came down the hatch. Watch out for people dressing and cooking, and remind them to take care over the sections that were pinned to the floor. The occasional trip on deck to help with a sail change offered only low grey skies, or fog, or darkness. We were conscious of Lisa and Keryn pulling battery and alternator systems apart, but we let them get on with their job, and trusted that they would turn up trumps.

I'm not sure what time it was when we finally had the rip fixed and the luff tape back on. It must have been late in the second day of the repair. I can remember that I was very tired, but happy that we were into the final stage of the job – until I saw the full size of the hole. I suppose that we had seen it growing as the sail came back together around the missing section. But it was only when we first had the rest of the sail together and tried to lay it out that we allowed the realisation to dawn. 'It looks bigger than we thought,' said Katie, which was something of an understatement.

I pulled out the tape measure, and we juggled the hole around the floor to measure it. 'About five and a half square metres,' I concluded.

'We can't use that much tape, we've still got the leech to fix,' replied Katie, measuring out the remaining spinnaker cloth. She looked up at me.

'Plan B,' I said.

'I guess we'll have to,' she replied. When the boat had been built, we had used as much spinnaker cloth as possible for things like locker covers and screens – with just this situation in mind. Now the scissors and knives came out, and we tore through the boat, reaping the harvest we had sown with our earlier planning. The pile of odd-shaped pieces grew impressively high. We would have enough material. But all the time the boat was sliding down the race track towards that forecast of A6 spinnaker sailing.

If putting the rip back together and the luff tape back on had been a laborious grind, then patching the hole was both more difficult and more subtle. We made up a section from our patchwork of materials first, then trimmed it roughly to shape. That was the easy part; the real problem was to fit the patch so that when the spinnaker was flying there were no tight spots. A tight spot is an area of cloth that loads up first when the sail fills. As the spinnaker gets more stressed the tight spot always has more strain than anywhere else. It's a weak point, the place where the sail will break early. In a sail loft you can lay the whole sail out flat, and it's easy enough to ensure that the cloth goes down evenly, that the repair takes up the right shape under load. When you can only work on half the patch at a time, the only way is to keep doing it over and over again. Each time you pin the sail down and tape the repair in place, you have to then lift it off the floor, hold it up and see how it looks. You must control your frustration at the knowledge that a job that was less than a day's work in a sail loft is creeping out towards thirty-six, then forty-eight hours. Not to mention the constant worry that the thing was going to look awful and blow apart the second it went back up. But finally we had to admit that we had done the best job that we could. It was ready to sew back together.

The sewing machine is a little twelve-volt beast that lives in the forepeak, except when it's breezy downwind, when he gets stowed aft. He screws into the sink, so that you can manoeuvre the sail around the galley. The sink is on the starboard side, and we were still reaching on starboard tack, so we could even keep our weight to windward while we were working on the sail. It's a good system – when you have the power. But Lisa had been as good as her word. They had figured out a way that we could use the sewing machine, but only while the generator was running and charging the batteries.

We had to juggle the resources carefully: we could only sew while we were charging, and we couldn't cook while we were sewing. To start with we worked on the leech tape in between the sewing sessions. As with the luff tape we had to unpick it first. Then we cut the leech back a little to get a clean edge, before stapling the tape back on with the leech cord in place. The tension on this was critical, or the sail wouldn't set properly. Then that, too, had to be stitched. All the sewing meant the sail wasn't getting fixed as fast as it might, but there was nothing we could do about that. At least we were still reaching, and didn't want to fly it yet. And after three days with barely any rest, the fact that we could no longer work around the clock meant that we could get some sleep. I was too tired to appreciate what a wonderful moment it was when we finally finished it. I fell into the bunk while Bridget packed the sail. It would be ready when we needed it. So long as it held together.

It took almost four days to repair the spinnaker. By then the low-pressure – which was supposed to bring the strong south-westerly – had picked up the back markers and swung north-east. The low moved at the same pace as Silk Cut and Chessie Racing, carrying them up to, then north of, the fleet denying the others the fast running conditions they had expected. The spinnaker stayed in its bag. It was never used in race conditions, and was only briefly hoisted at the stop-over in La Rochelle to assess the repair. It was replaced by a back-up sail for the final leg.

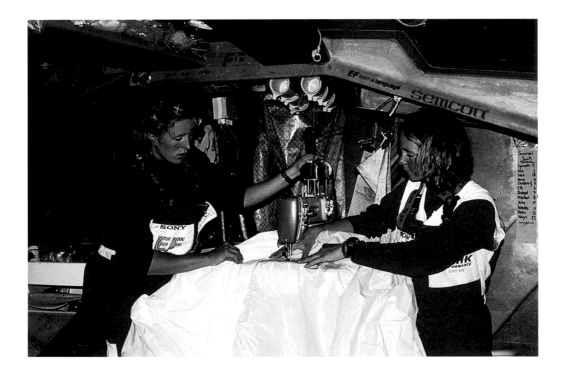

KATIE PETTIBONE (LEFT) AND ANNA DROUGGE SEW THE A6 IN THE FINAL STAGES OF THE MASSIVE REPAIR.

PREVIOUS PAGE AND ABOVE: THE NORTH ATLANTIC CAN BE JUST AS COLD AND WET AS THE SOUTHERN OCEAN.
AND AS DANGEROUS – THERE WERE MORE ICEBERG SIGHTINGS ON LEG EIGHT, THAN ON LEGS TWO AND FIVE.
ANOTHER TRIP TO THE TOP OF THE MAST TO ATTACH THE STROP TO THE SPINNAKER. (OPPOSITE)
NEXT PAGE: SETTING THE STAYSAIL INSIDE A REACHER IS A CLASSIC AND CRUCIAL WHITBREAD SAIL CONFIGURATION.

The northern charge of the back markers up the Leg Eight schedules was finally halted as everyone ran into a high-pressure ridge blocking the path to France. But the position of the ridge allowed Silk Cut and Chessie Racing to get closer to the finish. They had gone from two hundred miles behind to second and third place. But would the north continue to pay as the high pressure broke down? The strategists aboard EF Education, bolstered by Isabelle Autissier for that leg, thought so. Along with the leader Toshiba, they edged north. To the south, EF Language had covered every move that Swedish Match had made. They were one place in front, and they only needed to be a place behind to win the Whitbread. But now they were nervous; the light air of the high-pressure ridge threatened to turn the final few hundred miles into a lottery.

Magnus:

This was the second leg in succession that we had focused on staying close to Swedish Match. It was strange not to be concerned about winning the leg, just trying to beat one boat, but everyone had agreed that it was the only way to do it. Four days out from the finish we had Swedish Match one place behind us, between ten and twenty miles away. The situation was under control. The high pressure was the last unknown factor. No one knew quite how it would dissipate, whether the northern or southern boats would benefit, or if the whole fleet would go back into the mixer. As time went on the first thing that became clear was that the four northern boats would win the leg. With Swedish Match in the south, we would probably get our worst finish of the race – which was great! Because, with only five boats in our southern group, it was much harder for Swedish Match to gain the points that she needed. And the women

were looking good for a fourth. But there was still this huge area of light air between us and the finish.

Then suddenly we were through it. We still had our lead, we were into the filling breeze before Swedish Match, and the forecasts said there would be wind all the way to the finish. No one said anything, but a couple of days from La Rochelle we knew that it looked good. We all realised that something really unusual would have to happen for us to lose it now. It also helped that Merit Cup was ahead of us, with enough points to put Swedish Match under pressure for the overall second place. That meant that Gunnar could not afford to do anything radical. He had to sail straight to the finish, or risk losing a place to Innovation Kvaerner and Brunel Sunergy close at his heels, which would let Merit Cup get even closer overall. As the hours peeled away we slowly relaxed. The weather was mild, there was little chance of damage, we had a twenty-mile lead – it felt good.

It helped even further when the Race Office switched from six- to three-hour schedules. It was done for the media and spectators, but as Crusty said, 'We're match racing in the dark and every six hours someone turns the lights on.' Now they were flicking the switch every three hours; if Gunnar did make a move we would know about it before he could get too far. For the first time we didn't bother with the 'full-court-press' watch system for the end of the leg.

There was no need, and so everyone got a lot more sleep. We had time to clean the boat up too, so it was spotless – that was a first. We were also very happy for Education. As the northern boats did well, she looked certain to take fourth, which was fantastic.

We all had a lot of time to get used to the idea of winning. It was when I first started to think about the finish itself that I felt a sadness, an emptiness. And it hit me that the satisfaction is in the achieving, not the achievement. Like they say, it's the journey, not the arriving, that counts. And I suppose that was why there was no huge excitement as the hours ticked down towards the end. People were still sleeping off watch, just an hour away from the line. And even then, we were still very focused on the job, the trimming, the steering, finding the finish. Paul was working on the approach with Rudi, worrying about the sailing angles, lights, tide, windshifts. Crusty was steering, the breeze in the north-east. There was a bright moon to the south, orange lights stretching away along the coast, flat water; it was so quiet. So close to the finish and so quiet. And there it was, the finish line, between a blue flashing light and a white light on the Roche de Sud. Just a couple of hundred yards away.

Then we saw the first – and only – spectator boat. That was different too. In so many places the reception had been quite amazing. I will never forget Brazil, when we had arrived right in the middle of the Carnival. There'd been thousands of boats and people, an incredible party. And here we were, winning the race with a leg to spare – and there was just a single boat. That added to the atmosphere of quiet satisfaction, rather than wild excitement. I was so happy, I wanted to smile, then I couldn't stop smiling, but I didn't want to jump around and go crazy. And then the single spectator boat turned out to be our Team EF boat, driven by Johan. I remember I shook his hand as he came alongside, and said thank you. I think we both knew that in the future we would enjoy it more, but that for now it was enough to know that we had made it. The wild fear that something silly would take it away from us was finally gone.

Another thing that was different from the normal finish was that there was no Michael Woods, the Race Manager. He normally comes on board to check the seals that tie everything in place, like the propeller.

We didn't see him until we got to the dock, apparently his boat had broken down. But Johan had some of the wives and girlfriends on board; I saw Katy Worthington was one of those climbing over the guard-rail. And I felt sad that my family weren't there. I knew they wouldn't be, but even so... I wished I had pushed for them to come.

The boys lowered the headsail and put up eight huge EF flags instead. Roch Fortin from MTV Sweden came on board, he had been with us all the way around, making a documentary. Immediately Paul was being interviewed, and a few more press boats found us, and then it started to feel a little more like something had happened, that yes, we had won the Whitbread. But even then there was no sudden exhilaration or rush of victory: we had almost had too much time to get used to the idea. Josh steered us in, following the lead boat, and Johan kept transferring more journalists and film crews aboard, and soon

JOHAN SALÉN DELIVERED JOURNALISTS, GIRLFRIENDS, SUPPORTERS AND RINGING MOBILE PHONES
ONTO EF LANGUAGE AT THE FINISH.

there were people crowding the deck. But it still seemed a private thing. These were all friends, journalists that we knew well. They too had been on a journey, making their own, and sharing ours.

We were going to the fishing port, because there wasn't enough water in the main harbour. The fishing port is out of town, set deep in an industrial estate, and so even when we entered the harbour, the only people to greet our arrival were more press. And, of course, our amazing team. They put on a show; there were flares and flags and signs, horns, hooters and whistles. We nosed gently past Toshiba, Silk Cut, Chessie Racing, Merit Cup and, of course, EF Education – all lying silent – cutting through the glowing red smoke from the flares to shouted instructions from the dock. Then I could see that the women were still there. They were waiting with the shore crew, who had these crazy 'Paul Cayard' wigs and moustaches. I heard Paul shouting, gathering all ten Paul Cayards together to get their photo taken.

Before we knew it, everyone was there. The boat and the dock were heeling wildly, as people crowded

and reached from one to the other. There was the constant flicker of flashbulbs. Blur's 'Song 2' – our song all the way around the world – was playing somewhere, but it was almost drowned out by the laughter. There was such strong support from the girls on Education, they were so happy with their fourth, and our win. It was an incredible night for Team EF. Lynnath almost fell in as she tried to climb on board. Strong arms held her up, at a time when it's more traditional to throw people in. But it wasn't that kind of celebration. It was perhaps hard for the shore crew to understand, but the more relaxed mood suited us better. It was perfect that night, that feeling, with all those friends. Maybe there would be a big celebration in Southampton, with thousands of people and boats and all that stuff, but this night was for us, for everyone who had worked so hard.

There was no presentation of medals on the podium, no spraying the champagne like we had in every other port. We did have some photos taken up there, and that felt good. I felt that we were worthy winners, that we hadn't won it by anyone else's bad luck,

199

or by our good luck. Just by hard work. There was a press conference. That was the best one we ever did. The crew left the seat beside Paul for me, and that felt good too. Paul ran the press conference as only he can, and asked everyone the question, 'Will you do it again?' But who can really answer at a time like that? I remember looking over everyone's faces in the audience, then out of the back of the tent, watching the sun start to come up, and thinking: I'm sitting here and I've won the Whitbread.

And I suppose that was where this story should end, everyone driving off into La Rochelle, into the rising sun. Scraps of paper drifting across the old port in our wake, in the weak breeze and the soft light. Going for a big steak breakfast, and a new day in a different world, in a new kind of life where we, everyone involved with Team EF, could say we were people who had won the Whitbread, the last Whitbread. What an incredible journey it had been: almost thirteen years since the start of my first race, and now it was over. But there was one more thing that happened. I sat down and someone gave me a glass of wine, and I tried to ring home. But I guess many other people were ringing too; they were celebrating in Sweden, I know. The phone was engaged. And that's my only regret. That I never got through. That I didn't share that moment. It's easy to blame the wine, but I just didn't try hard enough. I hope I've made it up to them. To you, Margareta, Niklas and Joakim.

Ahead of the Team EF boats, Toshiba had saved her lead and salvaged some battered pride by moving north to cover Silk Cut and Chessie Racing. She led those two in to take her first leg win. Behind EF Education, Merit Cup had come in fifth, then the crucial pairing of EF Language and Swedish Match in sixth and seventh. Innovation Kvaerner and BrunelSunergy were the rearguard. The results meant that although the overall prize had been won, five boats could still take second and third overall. For Swedish Match, Merit Cup, Chessie Racing, Silk Cut and Innovation Kvaerner, success or failure for their 31,600 nautical miles of racing would depend on two days in the English Channel.

REACHING DOMINATED LEG EIGHT (ABOVE AND RIGHT).

NEXT PAGE: REACHING OFF THE GRAND BANKS IN ICE-COLD FOG.

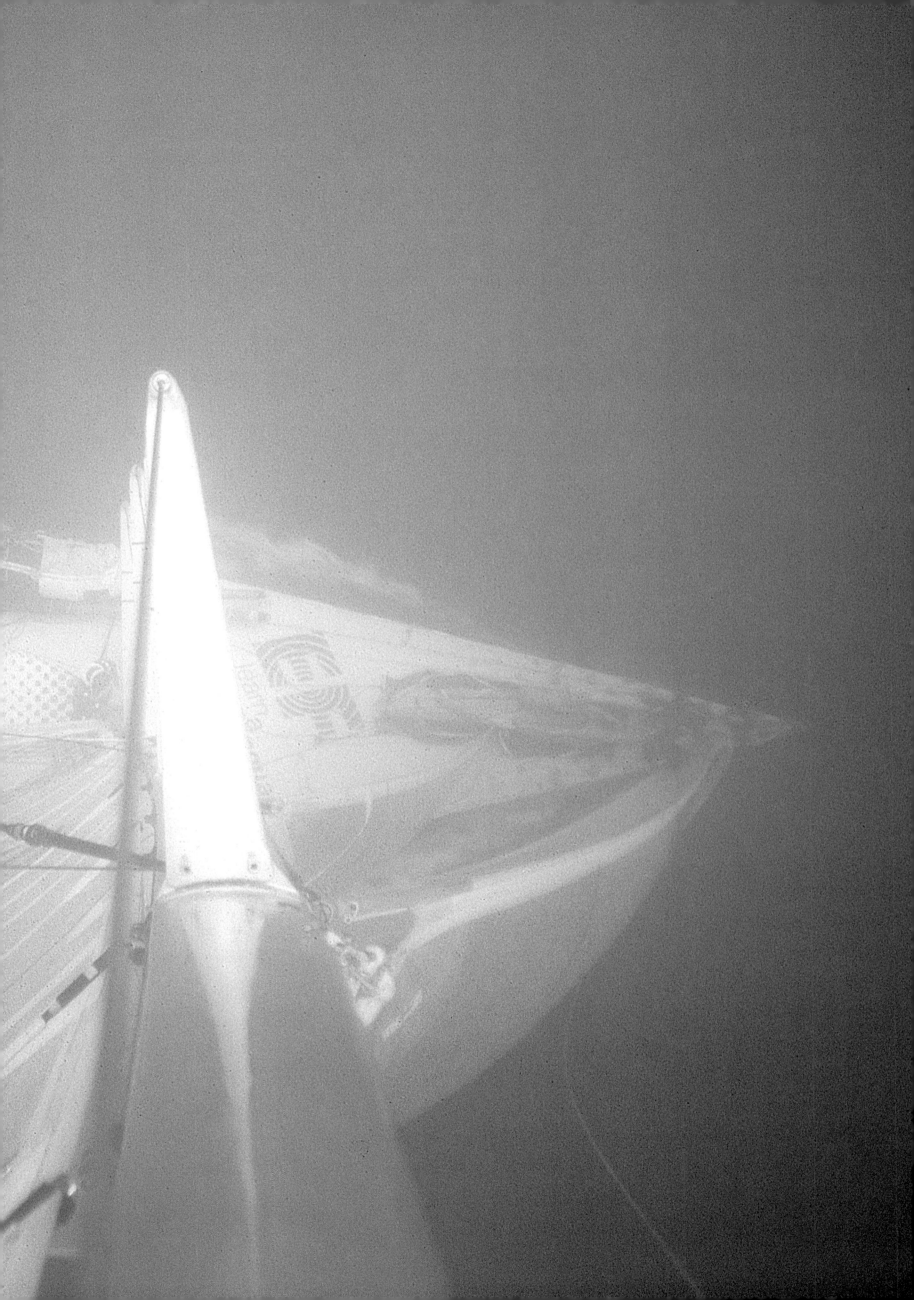

CHRISTINE GUILLOU AND PAUL CAYARD.

TEN 'PAUL CAYARDS' CELEBRATING PAUL CAYARD.

ANOTHER LAP

Although the Whitbread had been won, there was still the final leg to be sailed, the remaining podium positions to be settled. Leg Nine: 450 nautical miles up the west coast of France and across the English Channel, from La Rochelle to Southampton. Aboard EF Education they began the leg with high hopes of another success like the last. The two podium positions of BrunelSunergy on Legs Five and Seven meant that nothing could lift them off the bottom of the scoreboard overall. But they'd had a taste of what they could achieve, and this was the last chance to emulate that success.

It was a quick ride across the Bay of Biscay, reaching in a north-easterly that was gusting up to thirty knots. Things slowed dramatically at Ushant when the wind dropped and the fleet squeezed together into an unforgiving foul tide. The boats crawled round the north-west corner of France, until the tide turned and the wind started to shift to the north. The fleet tacked to port, and could soon lay the course. As the Dorset coast came into view, early on the morning of May 24, EF Education was trailing the fleet, eight miles behind the leader, and three miles behind eighth-placed Chessie Racing. They were close, but they had some work to do if they were to repeat their Leg Eight success.

Anna:

It was Lynnath who told us that they had extended the course, about two hours from Poole Fairway buoy.
Having sailed a lap of the world, we would have to do an extra lap of Christchurch and Poole Bay before they would let us back into the Solent to finish. The reason was that the arrival was timed for a television broadcast, and all the VIP and spectator boats. I had no idea then how big an impact this would have on us. We were reaching in towards Anvil Point in a light northerly breeze and smooth sea. It was a glorious summer morning, sunny, blue sky, crisp and cool. It was good to see England again, and the coastline that we had left behind us that autumn afternoon eight months before. The reach turned into a short beat once we rounded the headland and turned north up to Poole Fairway buoy. But once around that, we were reaching first to the east, and then back to the west across the bay. We changed the headsail and staysail to

212

the A3, or Code Zero, at North Head buoy, then set back off for Poole Fairway. The sun had disappeared, the sky had turned grey, these extra miles seemed so unnecessary. With Chessie Racing a couple of miles ahead, we had a further chance to catch them. But I think by then the mood was just to get finished. Perhaps some on board had that attitude before the start in La Rochelle. We hadn't sailed as well on this final leg. The extra spark that we had found on Leg Eight wasn't there.

It was when we passed North Head buoy the second time, and finally headed into the Solent, that I realised how the tide was building against us. It had been since the leaders had got through the narrow channel at Hurst Castle, the western entrance to the Solent, an hour earlier at the start of the ebb. It was almost midday, the sun desperately poking out from behind the clouds again, and the offshore northerly breeze was dropping as the sea breeze tried to fill in. Conditions couldn't have conspired against us to provide a worse scenario.

Hurst Castle is perched on the edge of a steep shingle beach, that sticks out from the northern mainland shore towards the Isle of Wight. It is a modern concrete and brick castle, of bunkers and gun emplacements, dating from the last century. There were people sitting on the beach, watching the last of the fleet sail into the Solent. And we were the

last of the fleet. But the tide was pouring out at up to four knots. With that much tide and the breeze dropping, even our Whitbread 60 was struggling to make any headway. We slipped past the first half of the castle, but the tide just got stronger. I couldn't believe it when we slowed and slowed, and finally stopped. Christine and Lynnath were calling for the anchor – the anchor! We had carried it all the way around the world and never even got it up on deck. And here it was, roped up and ready to go on the bow, with less than twenty miles to the finish line. Agonising. It was unbelievably frustrating. We didn't deserve this. We didn't deserve for such a few miles between us and the leaders to become such a huge gap. They were reaching towards home; we were trapped.

We didn't actually use the anchor; instead we wriggled and struggled back and forth across the channel, across the tide, going forwards, going back, trying the Isle of Wight shore, then the mainland. Trying to gybe into less current, holding in the shallow water as long as we dared. But there was so little tidal relief to be found, and nowhere could we make the breakthrough. For two hours we pushed up against this invisible wall, watched all the time by people on the beach, and the flotilla of spectator boats that hadn't carried on up the Solent with the leaders.

We were angry and frustrated. If it hadn't been for the extra lap, we could easily have beaten the tide. By

213

EF EDUCATION ONCE AGAIN SIGHTS THE ENGLISH COAST, AFTER EIGHT MONTHS OF RACING.

now we would be finished. And here we were – ridiculously stuck. But slowly little puffs of new wind started to find their way down the Needles Channel towards us, as the sea breeze announced its arrival. The invisible wall dissolved in fits and starts, as we got the new pressure and picked up speed. When it did finally fill in properly, the sea breeze came in strongly. Once through the narrow channel, the tide weakened and we started to roll off the miles. But as we cleared Hurst Castle, with eighteen miles to go, Merit Cup was only a couple of miles short of the finish line. For us, the race was over. It only remained to gybe our way down the Solent, to cross the line.

But the desperate atmosphere that had gripped us all when we were trapped melted away as we realised these were our last miles together. We dropped the spinnaker as we turned into Southampton Water, and put up a headsail for the final time, the final miles up to the final finish line. A beat against the tide. A struggle all the way around the world, and a beat against the tide to finish. There were some spectator

boats around us, although this was no armada – they had all followed Merit Cup, EF Language and the others in. At least we were getting there now, though not quite quickly enough – Lynnath reminded us, as we tacked up Southampton Water, that we had missed the window of time around high water that would allow us into Ocean Village.

It was so ironic; we had travelled so far to cross the line, but then had to finish our journey back to the pontoon we had left eight months previously on a powerboat. The final indignity. We took the sails down, and Fredde and Magnus came aboard to hold the boat in Southampton Water until they could get her into Ocean Village. Johan took us ashore in the Team EF's rigid inflatable.

Did it matter, once we were ashore? Yes and no. We were back, there were thousands of spectators, and it was finally like it was supposed to be. The homecoming. It was good to have finished. But those few miles that we were behind the others in the English Channel had turned into a great chasm, thanks to the

FOUL TIDE AND LIGHT AIR AT HURST CASTLE SERIOUSLY HINDERED PROGRESS. CALSHOT SPIT

MARKS THE ENTRANCE TO SOUTHAMPTON WATER.

tide at Hurst Castle. It had changed our experience. Instead of being part of a triumphant procession up the Solent, as we had expected, we had suffered those frustrating few hours, to limp in as tailenders. A heartbreaking anti-climax. But somehow that seemed to represent the whole of our project. For much of the time we had been so close, so near to the rest of the fleet. But the tiny differences had always been too much, and had become magnified into a gulf that we had only managed to cross once, on Leg Eight. For the rest of the time, we had been left watching from the back, close enough to touch, but without quite being able to grab and hold the race experience. And here, once again, a small difference had become a huge yawning gap, and we had been left with nothing to race for.

What was different about Leg Eight? It was largely the presence of Isabelle Autissier. She brought with her considerable extra experience, both in navigation and strategy. Her eight Atlantic crossings were a quarter of those completed by the other eleven of us combined. Only Leah and Marlene had sailed a Whitbread before and experience is vital in an ocean race, especially one as long and complex as this Whitbread. We had gained so much more of that experience by Leg Eight, and Isabelle helped it to work for us.

But we were extremely close to the other boats on so many other occasions, it needed so little extra to bring us up amongst them. I believe that the combination of lack of physical strength, and the lack of experience at the beginning, kept us from making that step earlier - and more often. And if we were so close on this race

with those limitations, what could we have achieved without them? I hope to find that out next time.

Ahead of EF Education, the overall results had been decided. The building foul tide had extended all the critical gaps between the boats after they rounded Poole Fairway for the first time. The differences at that rounding were tiny, but, for much of the fleet, those seconds were the margin between success and failure. Grant Dalton on Merit Cup had led EF Language at Poole Fairway by six minutes. And Language, the overall winner, was the first of the three boats that Dalton needed between him and Swedish Match to take second place overall. The second of those boats was Innovation Kvaerner, which was three minutes behind EF Language but only a minute ahead of Silk Cut. That was the boat Innovation Kvaerner had to beat by a single place to take fourth overall, pushing Lawrie Smith's crew into fifth overall. A further minute behind Silk Cut at Poole Fairway but the crucial four places behind Merit Cup, was Swedish Match – doomed to see second place overall slip from her grasp in the foul tide and light air of the Solent.

BrunelSunergy was sixth at Poole Fairway the first time, but Toshiba caught her before the finish. It **made no difference to their overall positions, Toshiba in seventh and BrunelSunergy in eighth. Chessie Racing trailed in eighth, and slipped to sixth overall. And while EF Language had won, EF Education had come last. After eight months, in nine legs and 31,600 nautical miles, the seventh and final Whitbread Race was over.**

THOUSANDS OF PEOPLE DESCENDED ON OCEAN VILLAGE TO BE A PART OF THE HOMECOMING AND THE VICTORY CELEBRATIONS.

MAGNUS OLSSON AS EF LANGUAGE CROSSES THE FINAL FINISHING LINE.

THE EF LANGUAGE TEAM LINE UP FOR PHOTOGRAPHERS AND THE PARTY BEGINS.

223

224

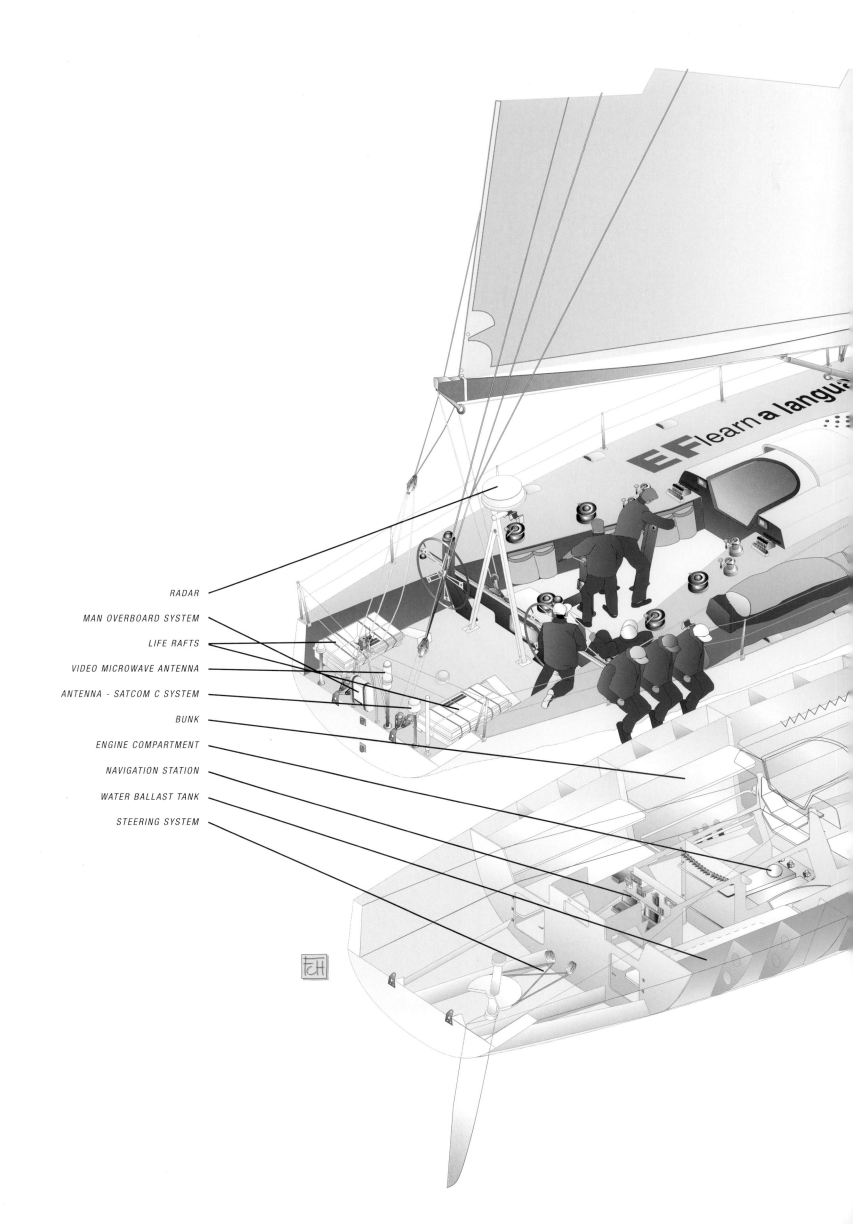

RADAR

MAN OVERBOARD SYSTEM

LIFE RAFTS

VIDEO MICROWAVE ANTENNA

ANTENNA - SATCOM C SYSTEM

BUNK

ENGINE COMPARTMENT

NAVIGATION STATION

WATER BALLAST TANK

STEERING SYSTEM

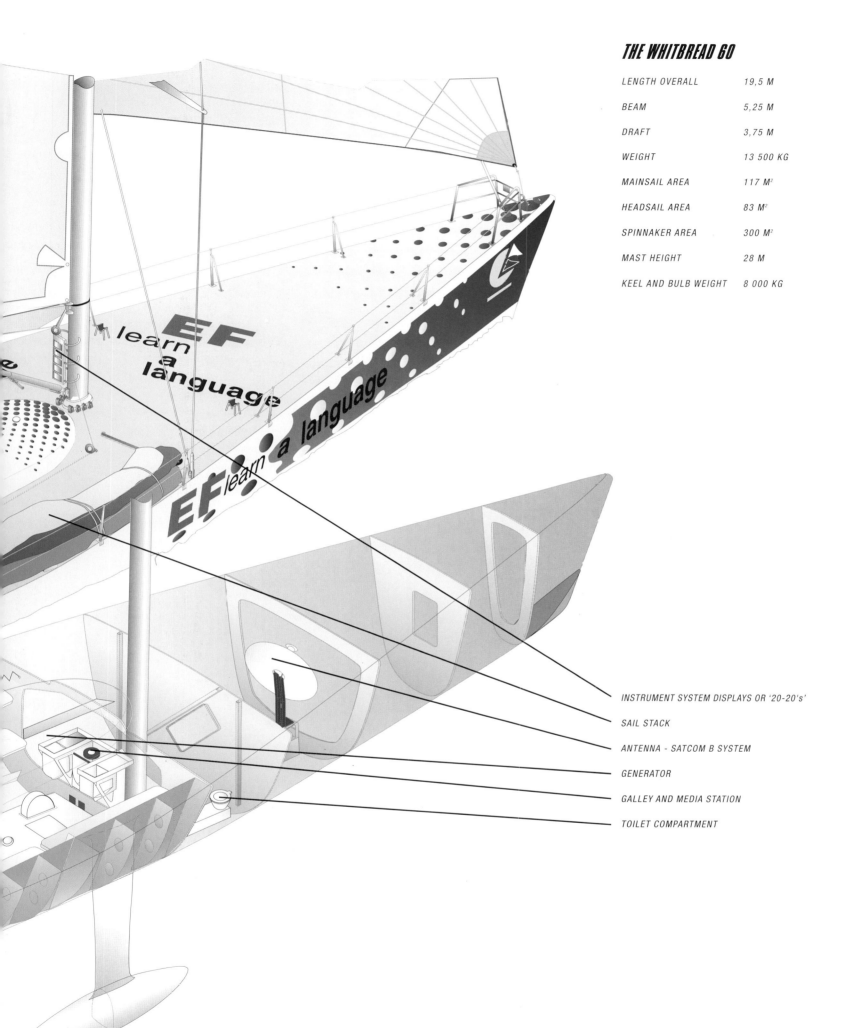

THE WHITBREAD 60

LENGTH OVERALL	19,5 M
BEAM	5,25 M
DRAFT	3,75 M
WEIGHT	13 500 KG
MAINSAIL AREA	117 M²
HEADSAIL AREA	83 M²
SPINNAKER AREA	300 M²
MAST HEIGHT	28 M
KEEL AND BULB WEIGHT	8 000 KG

EF learn a language

EF learn a language

INSTRUMENT SYSTEM DISPLAYS OR '20-20's'

SAIL STACK

ANTENNA - SATCOM B SYSTEM

GENERATOR

GALLEY AND MEDIA STATION

TOILET COMPARTMENT

225

1. MARK CHRISTENSEN
2. MARK RUDIGER
3. KIMO WORTHINGTON
4. CURT OETKING
5. MAGNUS OLSSON
6. CURTIS BLEWETT
7. PAUL CAYARD

8. JOSH BELSKY
9. JUSTIN CLOUGHER
10. STEVE ERICKSON
11. KLAS NYLÖF
12. CARL PALMSTIERNA
13. MATS ANDERSSON
14. MAGNUS RÅSTRÖM

15. JOHAN SALÉN
16. CARL FREDRIK BOKSJÖ
17. DAVE WHITE
18. GEORGINA HYDE
19. HELENA STENBORG
20. PIA JONSSON
21. VICTORIA STACEY

22. LOUISE PALMSTIERNA
23. ANDERS CARLBERG
24. ROGER BADHAM
25. CHRISTINE GUILLOU
26. KINY PARADE
27. LYNNATH BECKLEY
28. JOAN TOUCHETTE

29. KATIE PETTIBONE
30. LISA CHARLES
31. ANNA DROUGGE
32. CHRISTINE BRIAND
33. LEAH NEWBOLD
34. BRIDGET SUCKLING
35. KERYN MCMASTER

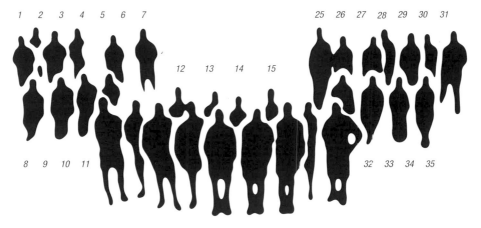

1 2 3 4 5 6 7   25 26 27 28 29 30 31

12 13 14 15

8 9 10 11   32 33 34 35

16 17 18 19 20 21 22 23 24

EF LANGUAGE

PAUL CAYARD (USA), SKIPPER

This was Paul Cayard's first Whitbread. He is perhaps most easily identified with the America's Cup, most notably in 1992 in San Diego, as skipper of Il Moro di Venezia – the Italian boat that won the right to challenge. In the 1995 America's Cup Paul was helmsman/strategist on Stars and Stripes/Young America – the defender. That was his fourth America's Cup. Cayard also counts the Star World Championships in 1988 amongst his many regatta wins.

MARK 'RUDI' RUDIGER (USA), NAVIGATOR/HELM

This was also Mark Rudiger's first Whitbread Race. Although he worked with Chris Dickson's 1993/94 Tokio syndicate, as sail-testing co-ordinator, system designer and navigator, he didn't sail the race. In the double-handed Transatlantic in 1990, Rudiger finished first in class – after navigating without electronics from Day Two! He is a veteran of 100,000 ocean miles in both mono-hulls and multi-hulls.

MAGNUS OLSSON (SWEDEN), WATCH CAPTAIN

Magnus Olsson's name is synonymous with the Whitbread for many people in Sweden. But like many top sailors, Magnus started out in dinghies – OKs, 505s and Lasers. He was the Swedish 505 Champion in 1974 and 1975, before he went on to compete in two America's Cups, and won three 6 Metre World Championships with Pelle Pettersson. His first Whitbread was onboard the English boat Drum, owned by pop star Simon Le Bon. In 1989/90, he was co-skipper of The Card, a Maxi ketch, together with Roger Nilson. In 1993/94 Magnus was on Intrum Justitia as watch captain – the second-placed Whitbread 60. On board EF Language he was responsible for the mast, boom, standing rigging and the clock. He was also Sailing Director for Team EF.

KIMO WORTHINGTON (USA), WATCH CAPTAIN

Kimo Worthington is another American, first-time Whitbread sailor, but again brought enormous experience to EF Language from all other areas of the sport. He's competed in four America's Cup campaigns. Kimo was responsible for knowledge of, and compliance with, all the various rules: the sailing instructions, notice of race, collision regulations, racing and measurement rules.

STEVE 'STEVIE' ERICKSON (USA), HELM

Another first-time Whitbread sailor. Stevie won his Olympic Gold Medal with Bill Buchan in the Star Class in 1984. His Star sailing career continued in 1985 with a World Championship win with Buchan, and in 1988 the same title with Paul Cayard. Other victories include the Maxi Worlds in 1988/89; International 50 Worlds in 1991; the 1995 Admiral's Cup and the Tour de France in 1996. And all that's without mentioning the three America's Cup campaigns. Stevie took care of all the food and clothing used aboard EF Language during the race.

MARK 'CRUSTY' CHRISTENSEN (NEW ZEALAND), HELM

Mark has one previous Whitbread Race to his credit, as trimmer and medic aboard the Whitbread 60 Winston in the 1993/94 Race. In preparation for that Whitbread, Winston finished second in the Fastnet Race and won the New York–Southampton Race, before finishing fourth in the Whitbread itself. Prior to that Mark sailed with the 1992 New Zealand Challenge for the America's Cup, part of his career as a match racer. He brings enormous offshore experience to EF Language – and a reputation as one of the world's fastest heavy air, downwind drivers. Mark was responsible for safety equipment and, as part of the sail development team, giving feedback to the sail designer and co-ordinating the sail inventory board.

KLAS 'KLABBE' NYLÖF (SWEDEN), MAST

Like Magnus, his fellow Swede aboard EF Language, Klas Nylöf started his sailing career in dinghies. In Klas's case it was Europes and 470s, before moving on to bigger boats. Until he was fifteen the sport of table tennis dominated his life; at one stage he was ranked third in Sweden. But after finishing school, Klas became a professional sailor. Within a couple of years he had crossed the Atlantic six times, and progressed quickly to managing several Swedish big boat projects. On EF Language he was one of the medics and, as engineer, responsible for all the mechanical systems.

JOSH BELSKY (USA), MAST

Josh Belsky is another American, another Whitbread first-timer, with another long list of sailing accomplishments from the professional circuits. These include sailing aboard Matador 2, winner of the 1991/92 Maxi World Championships. During the same period he won a J24 World Championship, and sailed with the successful defender of the 1992 America's Cup, America 3. As a result of this run of successes, Josh was voted Crewman of the Year by Sailing World Magazine in 1992. His second America's Cup was with the 1995 defender, Stars and Stripes/Young America. Josh had overall responsibility for EF Language's maintenance, and specific charge of the winches.

CURTIS BLEWETT (CANADA), BOW

Curtis Blewett's sailing has taken him through 30,000 nautical miles of Atlantic and Pacific racing, and seven ocean transits – but not a Whitbread. These miles have included the 1997 Miami–Jamaica Race on the ILC 70 Sayonara, and a comprehensive set of inshore regattas. Curtis is a rigger by trade, specialising in running rigging and Kevlar construction. As such, he was responsible for those things on board EF Language.

JUSTIN 'JUGGY' CLOUGHER (AUSTRALIA), BOW

Justin Clougher is a Tasmanian who also began in sailing dinghies, and moved on to notch up well over 100,000 nautical miles of ocean passage racing, which culminated in building and racing aboard the 1996 IMS Maxi Boomerang. Boomerang was the outright winner in the Newport–Bermuda Race, Kenwood Cup, San Francisco Big Boat Series and the Jamaica Race. This was his first Whitbread. Justin has an electrical/electronics background, and on EF Language he was responsible for the electrical and media systems, as well as being one of the two medics.

MARCO CONSTANT (SOUTH AFRICA), TRIMMER

Marco Constant is a Whitbread third-timer, having previously competed on Atlantic Privateer in the 1985/86 Race, before helping to sail Intrum Justitia to second place during the last Whitbread. Marco grew up sailing dinghies and keelboats, before studying architecture and completing three years compulsory national service. After that he embarked on his career as a sail-designer and trimmer. Marco has chalked up a long list of successes: 1993 and 1997 Admiral's Cup wins; the 1994 Kenwood Cup; the 1995 Mumm 36 European Circuit and the 1996 Mumm 36 World Championships; along with the 1996 Sydney–Hobart, 1994 and 1996 Cape Town to Rio race wins on board Morning Glory. Marco was part of the sail team, with responsibility for all the on-board repair.

CURT OETKING (USA), HELM/TRIMMER

Curt Oetking sailed on all but the second leg of the race, where he was replaced by photographer Rick Tomlinson. The sixth American Whitbread first-timer, like Paul Cayard, his America's Cup experience dates back to 1983 when he sailed on board Courageous. In 1987 he joined the crew of America 2, and in 1992 was with Cayard as a member of the Il Moro di Venezia team. Curt was with Chessie Racing between April and August in 1997, when he was responsible for organising the yacht's programme. On EF Language, he looked after the deck hardware.

PAUL MURRAY (NEW ZEALAND), TRIMMER/SAILMAKER

Paul Murray was the sailmaker during Team EF's preparation, and for the duration of the Whitbread Race. Paul came to Team EF from North Sails and the 1995 America's Cup, when he was a sailmaker for Team New Zealand, who successfully challenged and took the Cup back to Auckland. He has sailed extensively on the professional circuit, and was brought aboard EF Language for Leg Eight, when a broken wrist prevented Marco Constant from sailing.

RICK TOMLINSON (ISLE OF MAN), TRIMMER/PHOTOGRAPHER

This was Rick's fourth involvement with the Whitbread Race, which started by joining the Maxi Drum as a boat-builder and trimmer for the 1985/86 Whitbread. He started taking photographs aboard Drum and has continued ever since, becoming one of the world's best-known sailing photographers. His work has almost single-handedly defined the public's perception of the Whitbread over the last decade. In 1989/90 he raced aboard The Card, and in 1993/94 he was with Intrum Justitia. Rick sailed aboard EF Education for Leg One, and EF Language for Leg Two.

EF EDUCATION

CHRISTINE GUILLOU (FRANCE), SKIPPER

Christine Guillou is the latest in a long line of great French women sailors. Although this was her first Whitbread, her vast offshore experience includes two single-handed Figaro Races, in 1990 and 1991 on Groupe LG and Coup de Coeur Cherbourg respectively. In 1994 she was first in class on the mono-hull 60 Cherbourg Technologies, in a transatlantic double-handed race with Halvard Mabire as her co-skipper. She then raced in the Transat AG2R Lorient–St Barth with Christine Briard, aboard the Figaro one design Sill la Potagere. In 1995 Christine sailed with all-female crews in the Tour de France a la Voile, on the thirty-five-foot one design L'Oreal, and in the Round Europe Race on the multi-hull Whirlpool.

LYNNATH BECKLEY (SOUTH AFRICA), NAVIGATOR

Lynnath Beckley is a marine scientist from Durban, and much of her twenty years and 60,000 miles of sailing experience has revolved around the major regattas and ocean races in the South African sailing calendar. Lynnath has sailed primarily as a navigator and collected wins in the Cape to Uruguay in 1985, the Double Cape Race and Agulhas Race on numerous occasions, and the Da Gama Race in 1997. In the late 1980s, she was awarded a string of yachting honours from the University of Cape Town and the Royal Cape Yacht Club.

LEAH NEWBOLD (NEW ZEALAND), WATCH CAPTAIN

Leah started racing at eighteen, but did not get serious about it until she was twenty-three. Her international offshore experience started in the 1993/94 Whitbread Race, when she sailed aboard Heineken – the second time in the race's history that there had been an all-female crew. Subsequently, Leah was a member of the all-female crew in the 1994 Sydney–Hobart race. The following year she sailed to second as a skipper in the New Zealand Women's National Keelboat Championships; and first in class on general handicap in the Air New Zealand Regatta. Leah attended to the mast and standing rigging maintenance.

KINY PARADE (SWITZERLAND), WATCH CAPTAIN

Kiny Parade also began her competitive sailing in dinghies, which she came back to in 1996 as the Swiss Olympic coach for the Europe Class. But her professional sailing career started in earnest in 1991 when she won the Swiss Championships in the Surprise class. Since then Kiny has sailed in the Transat Quebec–St Malo with an all-female crew aboard Whirlpool. Kiny worked on the Challenge Oceanes Whitbread project before joining Team EF, and is also working on a single-handed challenge for the Figaro Race. Kiny's responsibility afloat was the deck hardware.

LISA CHARLES (USA), MAST

Lisa Charles has competed in everything from a Melges 24 to the Maxi boat Longobarda, and raced in most of the major regattas around the world. She also sailed in the first ever women's team in the America's Cup in 1995. Lisa was also responsible for the maintenance of America 3's two IACC yachts. In between and before

joining Team EF full time, Lisa worked on Tracy Edwards' Royal & SunAlliance Jules Verne Challenger, and was part of their team in the 1997 Transatlantic Challenge. Lisa was the engineer aboard EF Education.

KERYN MCMASTER (NEW ZEALAND), MAST

Keryn McMaster was sailing before she could walk, and her family runs the oldest sailmaking business in New Zealand. Keryn sailed in the 1996 Kenwood Cup onboard the Mumm 36 Georgia Express and in the Asia Pacific Mumm 36 Regatta where they finished third. In 1995 she sailed as part of an all-female crew in the Sydney–Hobart race. Keryn is a registered nurse and was the medic aboard EF Education, and also responsible for the safety equipment.

ANNA DROUGGE (SWEDEN), TRIMMER

Anna Drougge began sailing Optimists and Lasers at the age of ten, and after training as an electrical power engineer she turned to sailmaking. Gathering a lot of experience on yachts in various inshore and offshore races in Scandinavia, she then helmed an Express on the inshore circuit between 1990 and 1993. In 1993 and 1994 she also skippered yachts in the Round Gotland Race. In the summer of 1995 Anna joined Sony, the Whitbread 60 that had been Intrum Justitia. Sony finished third in its class in the Round Gotland Race in 1995. She was a member in the winning team in the Round Gotland Race in 1996. Anna was the on-board sailmaker for EF Education.

KATIE PETTIBONE (USA), TRIMMER

Katie Pettibone grew up sailing all types of boats in the Great Lakes region. Katie was part of the America 3 Foundation team in the 1995 America's Cup. In Europe she has competed in the Brut Cup Faberge Series in France, the Coppa dei Campioni D'Altura in Italy as well as the Tour de France a la Voile. Katie was the sail co-ordinator aboard EF Education.

BRIDGET SUCKLING (NEW ZEALAND), BOW

Bridget Suckling is a graduate of the Royal New Zealand Yacht Squadron Youth Scheme, and represented Wellington in the New Zealand Women's Nationals at sixteen. She went on to win the New Zealand Women's National Keelboat Championships in 1992 and 1994. In June 1996, after the ILC 40 World Championships in Greece, she joined the all-female crew aboard EF Education and was a member of the winning team in the Round Gotland Race a month later. Bridget attended to all the food on the boat.

MARLEEN CLEYNDERT (NETHERLANDS), BOW

Marleen Cleyndert also has a dinghy sailing background, mainly in the Optimist and 420 classes. She moved into keelboats at the age of sixteen and, after racing in J24s with all-female crews, joined the all-female crew aboard Heineken for the last four legs of the 1993/94 Whitbread Race. Marleen was responsible for the running rigging.

ALL THE ABOVE SAILED EVERY LEG OF THE WHITBREAD ABOARD EF EDUCATION, WHILE THE FOLLOWING SAILED ON ONE OR MORE LEGS, TO MAKE UP THE CREW NUMBER TO THE MAXIMUM OF TWELVE.

CHRISTINE BRIAND (FRANCE)

Christine is one of France's top women helms. Her sailing career spans twenty years of racing, in everything from 470s to yachts and multi-hulls. With six World Championship titles to her name, Christine has also sailed a lot of offshore miles. She was navigator and tactician on Ecureuil Poitou–Charantes, and finished second in the Open UAP 93 with Isabelle Autissier. Christine also sailed the Transat AGR2 in 1994 on Figaro Beneteau with Christine Guillou and finished fifth in the Open UAP 95 on the multi-hull Whirlpool, also with Christine Guillou. Christine sailed aboard EF Education on Legs One, Three, Four, Seven, Eight and Nine.

JOAN TOUCHETTE (USA)

Joan Touchette has extensive big boat experience. She worked with the Elle Racing Whitbread campaign as training skipper/watch leader for the 1997/98 Whitbread Round the World Race. Recent regatta successes include the Mumm 30 Class at Key West Race Week in 1996, the Melges 24 regatta in Los Angeles in 1995, and the Sonar Class in the International Women's Match Racing regattas at Marblehead and St Petersburg in 1995. Joan joined the crew for Legs Two, Three, Four, Five, Six and Seven.

ISABELLE AUTISSIER (FRANCE)

Isabelle Autissier is another French sailor with enormous offshore experience. Building her first yacht in 1987, the ten-metre sloop Parole, Isabelle finished third in the 1987 Mini-Transat. Isabelle moved on to the single-handed Figaro Race in 1988 and 1989, and was then seventh in the 1990/91 BOC Challenge, a single-handed round the world race. She beat the New York–San Francisco record in 1994 in 62J, knocking fourteen days off the existing time. Isabelle was aboard EF Education for Legs Eight and Nine.

MARIE-CLAUDE KIEFFER (FRANCE)

Marie-Claude has many thousands of racing and delivery miles to her credit which includes four single-handed Figaro Races. Marie-Claude sailed on board Heineken in the 1993/94 Whitbread as sail coordinator, trimmer and helm. She joined the crew of EF Education for the fifth leg from Auckland to São Sebastião.

EMMA WESTMACOTT (BRITAIN)

Emma sailed as watch captain, helm and engineer aboard Elle Racing's Whitbread 60, on their training voyage from England to Australia prior to the 1997/98 Whitbread. Emma then joined Tracy Edwards' Royal & SunAlliance for their Jules Verne Challenge, as watch captain and helm. Prior to that she had gathered over 80,000 miles in racing and chartering yachts. Emma sailed the second leg.

MELISSA PURDY (USA)

Like Lisa and Katie, Melissa is a veteran of the America 3 Foundation team in the 1995 America's Cup: she was the mainsheet trimmer aboard Mighty Mary. She was an All American woman sailor and college team racing champion, and lists the J24 World Championship amongst her regatta successes. More recently she has focused on match racing and winning all the US women's match racing events in 1996. She was aboard EF Education for the sixth leg.

Team EF knew exactly what they wanted in the construction of their two Whitbread 60s – quality, precision and a limitless attention to detail. To achieve these exacting standards, necessary for total confidence in the performance of the boats, Team EF needed direct control over the construction process. The best solution was to set up an in-house building team, in Sweden, rather than going to a commercial boat building company somewhere else in the world. But there were several problems: setting up a construction facility for just two boats could have been prohibitively expensive; and where would they find the necessary skills and knowledge in hi-tech composite construction?

Richard Gillies and Tim Smyth provided the technology solution. They are two New Zealanders with substantial reputations for running exactly the kind of construction programme that Team EF envisaged. They had built boats for every major international event – the America's Cup, the Whitbread and the Admiral's Cup. And constructed them all by setting up a new facility, using local skills, subcontractors and suppliers. Team EF would provide all the materials, equipment and the workforce; and Richard and Tim would ensure that the boats were built to the highest possible standards, to Team EF's precise specifications. But that was only half of the solution, they still needed somewhere to work. The city of Gothenburg had the answer – offering, rent-free, the use of part of the city's former shipyards. The huge shed was the ideal place to build the boats. Local businesses came up with more in-kind support, and the whole city got behind Team EF in its quest to build the perfect Whitbread 60s.

The two boats were built in a sandwich construction – two pre-impregnated layers of Kevlar fibre are stuck on either side of a layer of PVC foam, using an epoxy-resin glue. The pre-impregnated resin and fibre is cured at a higher temperature than conventional 'wet' resins, and the simple rule with epoxy-resin is that the higher the cure temperature, the stiffer the finished product. But it's perhaps the most difficult of modern composite construction techniques, because of the gas the PVC foam gives off when it is heated. This gas tries to 'blow' the two fibre layers of the sandwich off, just when it is absolutely critical that they stick. But Gillies and Smyth had researched special techniques to solve the problem – and they worked beautifully. Construction began in September 1996, and throughout the building process quality was the sole priority. The main hull took almost three weeks to lay-up. In contrast, a commercial boat builder might have to do it in a week, with the more pressing parameters of price and profit. The extra time ensured that the minimum material weight was used for the strongest possible structure - the key to a fast Whitbread 60.

The people of Gothenburg were involved at every stage. As well as the local work-force and suppliers, a free-standing balcony and video lounge were constructed inside the building facility, and up to 20 or 30 people visited each night. They were shown the boat building process, and short films to explain other aspects of the Team EF project and the Whitbread Race. Other Swedish manufacturers were also involved, Ka-Me-Wa for instance built the keel, milled from high-grade Swedish stainless steel. May 1997 was when the two Whitbread 60s were finally finished, launched by the King and Queen of Sweden, and ready for their round-the-world voyage.

TEAM EF'S TWO WHITBREAD 60s TAKE SHAPE IN A VAST FACTORY IN GOTHENBURG.

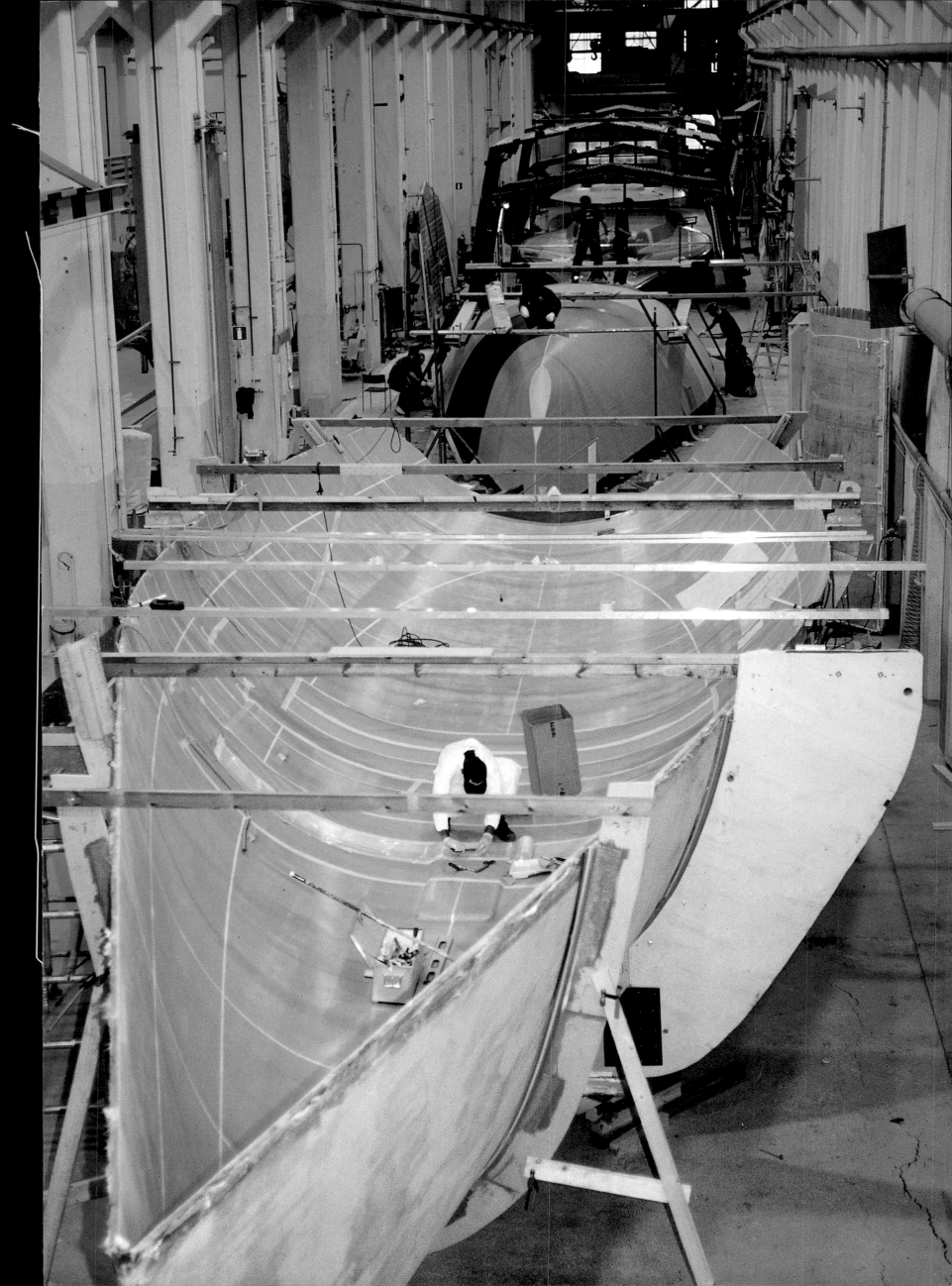

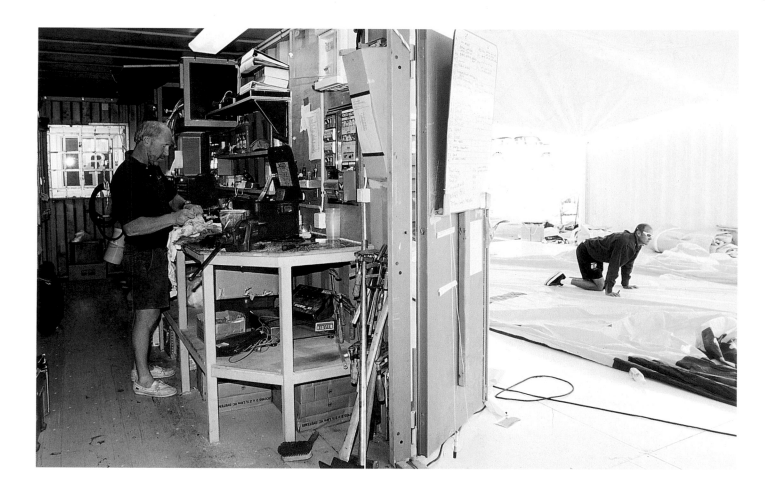

Two boats race around the world, to nine stop-over ports in seven countries. At each port, both boats must be completely overhauled. Each system has to be taken apart, checked, analysed and perhaps modified as a consequence of any lessons learnt. Organising the support team – the equipment, technology and skills – to make this happen is no small task.

When Team EF set about creating the structure and systems for their shore programme there were two over-riding, interlocking principles. First, they should be self-sufficient for all maintenance and upgrade work, both in skills and equipment. Team EF's goal was to require no more from each stop-over than a piece of flat ground and a crane. That would give them a level of control over costs and time management that was unachievable if local boatyards were relied on. And second, the team should create a single support centre in each port. The offices, workshops and sail-loft would all be in one place, as near the boat as possible.

Team EF felt there were clear-cut logistical advantages to one workplace. In the normal run of things people only need to get from the accommodation to the boat. That cuts down on transport cost and organisation. And with the office near the dock and workshops, there are rooms, phones, faxes and computers readily available for people who need to contact suppliers, order parts, make plans or just talk something through. There's another advantage, it's the open office principle – half-overheard conversations at the coffee machine are as important a part of efficient communication and operation as memo writing. Put everybody to work in the same place, and you get that crucial, informal communication network.

The first stage in making this happen was bringing together a group of people with the right mix of skills and experience to do any job, to cope with any eventuality in the nine long months. The second stage was to provide them with the equipment and facilities to do those jobs.

A system was planned where two sets of two forty-foot containers would be shipped around the world. The first set went from Southampton to Cape Town, then leap-frogged three stop-overs to go to São Sebastião in Brazil, then another two stop-overs to go to La Rochelle, before returning to Gothenburg. The second set also commen-ced their journey in Southampton, but set off directly to Fremantle, then going by train to Sydney and on to Auckland by sea. From there they went to the United States – Fort Lauderdale, Baltimore and Annapolis – before completing their journey back to Southampton.

The two sets of containers held an almost identical inventory of equipment: tools, paint, resins, Kevlar fabric, sails, food, video-conferencing unit, boat cradle, vacuum cleaners, dehumidifiers, fridges, BBQ and kitchen uten-sils, more nuts and bolts than you can imagine, silicones, electrical adapters, faxes, a photocopier and office equip-ment, personal bags, bikes and even surfboards. There were also two sets of spares for each of the systems on the boat – some of which would be returned to the manufacturers should they not be used. There were dif-ferences: the container that went to São Sebastião also contained a lathe and a milling machine, as the team were uncertain of the facilities in this tiny Brazilian port.

Then there were the items that could not be duplica-ted, the more expensive spare parts, and those that couldn't be returned to manufacturers. There were the crew's personal bags that had to be transported to meet them at each finish. Sails that were not being used on that leg. The specialist tool boxes of the different shore-crew members. Not to mention the phone system – Siemens provided the team with a switchboard that could run up to eighteen different extensions (the biggest challenge was to make it work in all seven stop-over countries – and Siemens succeeded). Although the team usually rented only six lines, they were high data rate transmission lines (ISDN) that could be used for the

video-conferencing unit. All this equipment had to be moved to each of the successive stop-over ports. For some journeys the equipment could be taken overland, which was a substantial saving. But about two to four thousand kilos of air freight had to be transported be-tween four stop-overs: Cape Town to Fremantle; Auckland to São Sebastião; São Sebastião to Fort Lauderdale; Annapolis to La Rochelle.

Once in the stop-over port, everything had to be set up ready for the arrival of the boats. The team usually rented two twenty-foot containers (one of which was refrigerated) and the equivalent of two more forty-foot containers as office space. These were all built into a compound that allowed the construction of the sail-loft in the middle. A canopy was erected – as much for shade as for protection from rain – and a specially built wooden floor laid that allowed the sailmakers to work.

Then there was the support structure for the support team – accommodation and transport that allowed all these people to work and live happily and efficiently. Two chefs travelled with the team. They cooked lunch and dinner so that people could eat together, rather than apart in different restaurants. This meant that the crew's diet and nutrition could be much more precisely control-led than if it had been left to whim and local restaurant menus. Restaurant meals also tend to be time-consum-ing, and their hours restrictive. Another Team EF priority was always to choose apartment accommodation rather than hotels, if at all possible. Then breakfast and snack facilities were available to the team, and those families and children travelling with them.

And finally, all this had to be managed and operated on a day-to-day basis. Ultimately, the principles and ideas were made to work by people, by individuals. It was those individuals who made the Team EF support programme such a success. The final plaudit? All they needed was the flat ground and the crane.

TEAM EF SHORE SUPPORT

RICHARD BRISIUS, SHORE MANAGER

Harbours, mooring, compound, training base, accommodation, freights, custom clearance arrival/departure immigration crews, vehicles and fuel, gym, laundry, setting up and packing up of on-site office and administration, office and container rentals, security, on-site cash flows, accounts, race emergencies, shore-support action plan, shore-team communications, WRTWR stop-over organisation communication.

TIM SMYTH, TECHNICAL MANAGER

Overall responsibility of maintenance of the racing boats when in port, setting up and packing up of containers and technical work areas, container power, contact with local boatyards, boat-lifting, boat-building, painting, technical support to boats while racing, supplier contacts, race emergencies, assisting with technical shore-support action plan.

DAVE WHITE, RIG SERVICE

Maintenance of the rigs, rig-lifting, service of deck fittings, metal works, dock set-up, power washer and electrical power, compound security, fencing and lighting, keys, assisting in setting up and packing up of containers and technical work areas.

PAUL MURRAY, SAILMAKER AND SERVICE LOFT CO-ORDINATOR

Service of sails, setting up and keeping in order service loft in each port (material, machines, awning and floor between containers), communication with local lofts, assisting in setting up and packing up of containers and technical work areas, sail maintenance budget.

SAM ROBERTS, SAILMAKER

Service of sails, setting up and keeping in order service loft in each port (material, machines, awning and floor between containers).

FIGGE BOKSJÖ, COMPUTER AND COMMUNICATIONS

On-board computers and networks support as requested by navigators, on-board electronics maintenance assistance as requested by navigators, shore-team computers support, Siemens phone system and phone lines onsite, office power, email access, technical database, setting up locally and updating, assisting in setting up and packing up of on-site office and administration.

MAGNUS RÅSTRÖM, TECHNICAL ASSISTANT/BOAT-BUILDING

Composite works, service of boats under Technical Manager's guidance, assisting in setting up and packing up of containers and technical work areas.

FREDDE NYLÖF, TECHNICAL ASSISTANT/WAREHOUSE

Maintenance and keeping of tools and spare inventory, incoming goods, organising container stowage areas for sails, boat equipment etc. (prior to boats' arrival), inventory control and security, touch-up painting, personal bag check-in and movements, service of boat under Technical Manager's guidance, assisting in setting up and packing up local technical set-up.

PIA JONSSON, CO-ORDINATOR

Team travel, flights, pick-ups, graphics on site, clothing distribution, inventory control on site, updating phone lists, updating schedule, on-site office supplies, local freights, courier, visas, project information, social events, assisting in setting up and packing up of on-site office and administration.

HELENA STENBORG AND MATS ANDERSSON, SHORE-CHEFS

Setting up and packing up of local cooking and dining areas, menu planning, cooking and serving of all food on shore, purchasing of food on shore, assisting on-board chefs with food on board, arrivals and parties, general service for crews, assisting in setting up and packing up of containers and technical work areas.

ANDERS CARLBERG AND CARL PALMSTIERNA

Branding

ROGER BADHAM, METEOROLOGIST

All weather research and forecasting prior to each leg, briefing and preparing the afterguard of both boats.

LOCAL KNOWLEDGE

SOUTHAMPTON:	SARAH O'KANE
CAPE TOWN:	ANTHONY SPILLEBEEN AND ROB SHARP
FREMANTLE:	ANDREW ANNANDALE
SYDNEY:	LINDSEY MARWOOD
AUCKLAND:	COURTENAY SUCKLING
SÃO SEBASTIÃO:	DANIELA GARCIA
LA ROCHELLE:	PATRICIA GOUBARD

Pick-ups, deliveries, mail and packages at the post office or via courier, daily shopping round, assisting the team members in sourcing parts and services.

TEAM EF

FRED ANDERSSON
Chairman

JAN LITBORN AND PETER NILSSON
Members of the board

JOHAN SALÉN
President

JASINTA RAJAN AND ANNA NYCANDER
Finance

MALIN GAVENAS AND CATARINA GÖTHE
Administration

MARIKA HJELM, GEORGINA HYDE AND VICKY STACEY
Press

MARINA DYFVERMAN KÖCK
Design

TOM LEVIN
Branding

LOUISE PALMSTIERNA
Events

MARIT SÖDERSTRÖM
Marketing

IN 1974 A WHITBREAD WINNER, TODAY A NICE CRUISING BOAT.

The evolution of the Whitbread Race is a tale that has been repeated throughout sport, a story of the transition from amateur challenge to professional achievement. This story began back in 1973/74, when the Royal Naval Sailing Association picked up on an idea that had been gathering momentum for some time; a fully crewed round the world yacht race. It's difficult now to realise how radical this idea was at the time. But it was only in the previous decade that Francis Chichester and others had established that yachts could even be sailed through the Southern Ocean and around the world – never mind raced.

Nevertheless, the RNSA found backing from Whitbread and Company Limited, and announced the first Whitbread Round the World Race in May 1972. Seventeen yachts started the first leg, nineteen took part in total and fourteen completed the course. That first course was from the Solent to Cape Town, Sydney, Rio de Janeiro and back to the original start line off Portsmouth. The fleet was comprised of standard racer/cruisers of the day, boats with white Dacron sails that hanked on to headstays, with fridges and bilges packed with food and good wine. Navigators worked by dead reckoning and sextant, and reported their position by 50-watt Single Sideband Radio once a week – or tried to. A Swan 65, ketch rigged and skippered by Ramon Carlin, won from the British Services' yacht Adventure. The results were decided on corrected time, under the old IOR rating system. But that first race was to cost three men their lives: all of them fell overboard and couldn't be found. Many questioned whether this was sport. Perhaps not, but fourteen boats had proved that yachts could race the clipper and square-rigger routes through the Southern Ocean. When the second Whitbread was announced, others would return and begin to reshape the challenge.

If the first Whitbread had been all about finishing,

the second started the long trend towards a focus on winning. Of the fifteen boats that arrived on the start line on August 27, 1977, many more of them had been purpose-built and designed. But these were still yachts that wouldn't look out of place in a Mediterranean anchorage. They had coachroofs and portholes, and were built from cold-moulded wood, aluminium and fibreglass. Radio position reporting was increased to twice a week, and the IYRU had to be asked to give special permission to allow the sponsors' names as boat names. It was a small step, but still a step in the direction of professionalism. The course had also been altered, again starting from Portsmouth and running to Cape Town, but going on to Auckland rather than Sydney, before Rio de Janeiro and back to the Solent. And the Whitbread had its first woman skipper, one of only four in its history, Clare Francis. It was won by Cornelis van Rietschoten and Flyer, a sixty-five-foot Sparkman and Stephens ketch. It was the first of two consecutive wins for van Rietschoten, and set the race on its path to its modern form.

For the 1981/82 race, van Rietschoten built a custom Maxi (maximum or 'Maxi' size of seventy feet of rating allowed under the IOR rating rule) yacht to win on both elapsed and corrected time – an objective in which he succeeded. He formed his crew early and spent the summer prior to the start training. There was a new professionalism at the front of the fleet. But of the twenty-nine yachts that competed (twenty finished), the majority were still production-built boats of a mix of sizes. It's hard to believe now, but an old 1977 Admiral's Cupper entered. It is difficult to imagine a modern IMS 48 doing the Whitbread – never mind a Mumm 36. The race was still an adventure at heart – even the specially built Flyer had an upholstered interior. One incident in 1977/78 had led to an enforced change of course: an exclusive party at the yacht club

in Rio had been gate-crashed by the crews. An official had overreacted, the riot police were called and tear gas and battens wielded. The Whitbread hasn't been back to Rio de Janeiro since then. The 1981/82 Race again left from Portsmouth, running to Cape Town and Auckland, but Mar del Plata in Argentina was substituted for Rio, before the fleet returned to Portsmouth.

As a result of the Falklands War, the course for 1985/86 was changed again, with Punta del Este in Uruguay being substituted for Mar del Plata. The fleet had a different look to it – fifteen yachts started and seven of them were at, or close to, Maxi rating. All of these boats were commercially sponsored, with the exception of Drum, owned by pop star Simon Le Bon. Many were crewed by professionals and came to the start line after months of training and preparation. The first Kevlar sails appeared, but no one dared take them into the Southern Ocean. Commercial pressures were starting to make themselves felt in other ways. It was a fifty-nine-foot French sloop, L'Esprit d'Equipe, that won the race on corrected time and took the main trophy. The backers of the Maxi yachts were not impressed, and for the 1989/90 Race, the Whitbread Trophy was to be awarded to the fastest elapsed time around the world, leaving the handicap event as a secondary prize. Not only did it ensure that the big spenders took home the major trophy, but the contest for it was simpler for a growing non-sailing audience to understand: first home wins.

Political pressure came to bear on the race too, and the course was changed once again – Cape Town was removed and Punta del Este served as a stop-over on both transits of the South Atlantic. Partly because of the considerable extra distance this added, another stop-over was introduced in Fremantle, returning the Whitbread to Australia for the first time since the debut race. And on the way home from Punta del Este, the

Whitbread visited Fort Lauderdale, bringing the event to the United States and its vast potential audience for the first time.

That new look 1989/90 race was won by a skipper who had competed in all five Whitbreads to date. Peter Blake led the New Zealand Maxi ketch Steinlager 2 to wins on all six legs and overall. It was a phenomenal achievement with which to bow out of an event that was changing more rapidly than ever. Seventeen of the twenty-three boats were Maxis or within a whisker of it. The Argos satellite system allowed daily position reporting, and the winners and losers were visible, even in mid-ocean, to an increasingly interested world. Tracy Edwards helped capture the imagination of a general audience by taking the first all-female crew around in the fifty-eight-foot Maiden Great Britain. But after all the changes and improvements in safety equipment, it was this race that saw the first fatality since 1973/74. Tony Phillips went overboard from Creightons. Naturally in the Southern Ocean. Although he was recovered, a remarkable enough endorsement of the improvements in both technique and equipment, he couldn't be resuscitated.

This tragedy was the exception, however; the adventure element was receding as the racing relentlessly gathered intensity. Nowhere was this better reflected than in the detailed attention to weight saving. Freeze-dried food had already made its appearance, now it was all you could find apart from a few chocolate bars. Many crew were restricted to a single book each, and such luxuries as Walkmans and their

tapes carried strict limits. Ramon Carlin's wine cellar, Flyer's upholstered interior – all were as distant a memory as the idea of taking the spinnaker down at night. But if the crews believed the 1989/90 race was intense, they had reckoned without the Whitbread 60, or Chris Dickson.

Whitbread PLC were running the 1993/94 race themselves, rather than merely sponsoring it. And the changes to make the race more accessible to its audience were legion – the course was about the only thing that remained the same. The race was now run in two classes, and for the first time there was to be no handicap prize at all – each class would be won by the first boat over the line. The Maxis were back, but nowhere near the numbers of four years previously (five came to the line and four finished). The main attention diverted to the new class, the ten Whitbread 60s. These boats had been invented to limit the rapidly escalating budgets, to keep them in proportion to the marketing returns of Whitbread racing. The Maxi ketches that had dominated the previous race were particularly voracious money-guzzlers, and their drop in numbers vindicated the birth of the new class.

The Whitbread 60 was smaller, more modern, with sail and construction limitations that kept the budgets to the necessary levels. It was also unbelievably demanding to sail. Almost as fast as the Maxis, the smaller boats had a much more violent ride. Dickson came along with an America's Cup-bred intensity, and now there was nothing on the boat that wasn't directly related to the racing – no books, no Walkmans, nothing.

You slept or you raced or you worked. The water ballast made the interior cramped, and the constant search for weight loss ensured that the crews managed to find even more gear that they could dispense with.

The satellites that allowed six-hourly position reporting meant a further step into the media-orientated future. Success and failure could be tracked by spectators world-wide, four times a day, through 'fax-back' facilities. Technology also allowed video and still footage to be sent off the boats during the leg. With minimum limits set as to how much was transmitted, the eyes of the world were focusing ever more clearly on the racers every move. Dickson led the 1993/94 event until his mast came down off Brazil on the fifth leg. Yamaha snuck through the Doldrums to Fort Lauderdale to reverse her deficit to the second-placed boat Intrum Justitia, and held the lead to the finish. In the Maxis, Grant Dalton led all the way around in New Zealand Endeavour.

The stage was set for the seventh Whitbread. Ten Whitbread 60s in an utterly single-minded pursuit of victory, crewed by professionals, funded from corporate marketing budgets. With the Internet and satellite transmission providing more and better coverage than ever, ocean racing had truly come of age as a professional sport. The final links with the past were being broken, it would be the last Whitbread, as the sponsor of twenty-five years sold the rights to the next race to the multinational Volvo. And the Maxis had done their last. This time there would be a single class, a single race, a single winner.

BAD WEATHER ISN'T CONFINED TO THE SOUTHERN OCEAN – THIS IS FLYER AT THE ENTRANCE TO THE SOLENT.

BRUNELSUNERGY · NED11 *DESIGNER: JUDEL/VROLIJK. BUILDER: HOLLAND COMPOSITES. SKIPPER: ROY HEINER .*
NAVIGATOR: STUART QUARRIE

From the beginning, BrunelSunergy was perhaps the underdog of this spectacularly well-qualified fleet. One of only two boats not designed by Bruce Farr & Associates at the start in Southampton, she also had a comparatively inexperienced crew. The original skipper Hans Bouscholte had never sailed a Whitbread before, though the rest of the crew could muster eight Whitbreads between them. Changes were made early in the race, with Roy Heiner and Stuart Quarrie joining the boat and, despite an equal lack of Whitbread experience, the changes made a difference.

CHESSIE RACING · USA60 *DESIGNER: BRUCE FARR & ASSOCIATES . BUILDER: GOETZ CUSTOM BOATS. SKIPPER: GEORGE*
COLLINS. NAVIGATOR: JUAN VILA

Chessie Racing was something of a dark horse, and mounted an unusual campaign, mostly because of the organisational structure. The only boat to be privately financed, by skipper George Collins, Chessie Racing carried a core crew but used an extended list of guests throughout the race. Key experience amongst the crew came from navigator Juan Vila, who sailed aboard Fortuna Extra Lights in 1989/90 and Galicia '93 Pescanova in 1993/94, and watch captain Grant Spanhake who was with Lion New Zealand in 1985/86 and Fisher & Paykel in 1989/90. Those who came and went included some very well-known names from the professional circuits, including Jim Allsopp, Gavin Brady, John Kostecki, Dee Smith and Mike Toppa.

AMERICA'S CHALLENGE · USA11 *DESIGNER: ALAN ANDREWS. BUILDER: GOETZ CUSTOM BOATS. SKIPPER: ROSS FIELD.*
NAVIGATOR: HALVARD MABIRE

America's Challenge had a mixed pedigree when she came to the start line in Southampton. She was skippered by Ross Field, winner of the
Whitbread 60 class with Yamaha in the 1993/94 event. And she had a high quality crew that included several others from that boat.
America's Challenge nevertheless struggled for funds to get to the start. Those funds dried up in Cape Town and she was withdrawn from
the race.

INNOVATION KVAERNER · NOR2 *DESIGNER: BRUCE FARR & ASSOCIATES. BUILDER: KVAERNER MANDAL. SKIPPER: KNUT*
FROSTAD. NAVIGATOR: MARCEL VAN TRIEST

Innovation Kvaerner had the youngest skipper in thirty-year-old Knut Frostad, with one Whitbread behind him, aboard Intrum Justitia in
1993/94. He surrounded himself with sailors of quality and experience, and the project acquired the 1993/94 W60 Winston as a training
boat. Navigator Marcel van Triest had already done the job twice, with Equity & Law in the 1989/90 race, and narrowly coming second with
Knut aboard Intrum Justitia four years previously. A third Intrum Justitia veteran was watch captain Pierre Mas, on his second Whitbread,
although he left the boat in Brazil, and was replaced by America's Cup and former Match Racing World Champion Ed Baird. Sail co-ordinator
Jim Close had been around twice before, having been with Chris Dickson's Tokio in 1993/94, when a dismasting cost them a race they were
comfortably leading.

MERIT CUP · MON7000 DESIGNER: BRUCE FARR & ASSOCIATES. BUILDER: MARTEN MARINE. SKIPPER: GRANT DALTON.
NAVIGATOR: MIKE QUILTER

Merit Cup came to the start line in Southampton as one of the race favourites. Led by five-time Whitbread veteran Grant Dalton, and with a two-boat preparation programme that began back in March 1997, this was a gilt-edged project. The depth of experience aboard was enormous. Dalton had skippered the winning Maxi, New Zealand Endeavour, in the previous race. Navigator Mike Quilter and watch captain Kevin Shoebridge had both done three previous races and won two of them: with Dalton in 1993/94, and Peter Blake's all-conquering Steinlager 2 in 1989/90. The rest of the crew could muster another five laps of the planet amongst them.

SILK CUT · GBR1 DESIGNER: BRUCE FARR & ASSOCIATES. BUILDER: MCCONAGHEY BOATS. SKIPPER: LAWRIE SMITH.
NAVIGATOR: STEVE HAYLES/VINCENT GEAKE

Silk Cut was another of the favourites at start time in Southampton, benefiting from the track record and experience of skipper Lawrie Smith. Smith, who had initially been with Team EF until leaving to join the British boat, had been round the world three times previously, most notably skippering Intrum Justitia to her second place in 1993/94. He took with him a mix of youth and experience, navigators Steve Hayles (Legs One, Two, Three and Four) and Vincent Geake (Legs Five, Six, Seven, Eight and Nine) had both been round once before, on Dolphin & Youth in 1993/94, and Rothmans (Smith's 1989/90 command) respectively. Watch captains were Gordon Maguire, also with Smith on Rothmans and watch captain aboard Winston in 1993/94, while Stuart Bannatyne was a helm on the winning maxi, New Zealand Endeavour, in 1993/94.

SWEDISH MATCH · SWE2000 *DESIGNER: BRUCE FARR & ASSOCIATES. BUILDER: COOKSON'S. SKIPPER: GUNNAR KRANTZ/ERLE WILLIAMS. NAVIGATOR: ROGER NILSON*

Skipper Gunnar Krantz and navigator Roger Nilson had been together through two other Whitbreads, on The Card in 1989/90 and Intrum Justitia in 1993/94, while co-skipper Erle Williams had been around once before in 1981/82, on the winner Flyer. Together with watch captain Tim Kroger, who was also on Intrum Justitia, and Rodney Ardern who was aboard Tokio in the same race, this was the core experience of a very well-prepared campaign. Matt Humphries, skipper of Dolphin & Youth in 1993/94, joined the boat in Cape Town after America's Challenge pulled out. Swedish Match used Heineken, another W60 from the 1993/94 Race, as a training boat in Sweden.

TOSHIBA · USA1 *DESIGNER: BRUCE FARR & ASSOCIATES. BUILDER: NEW ENGLAND BOATWORKS. SKIPPER: CHRIS DICKSON/PAUL STANDBRIDGE. NAVIGATOR: ANDREW CAPE/MURRAY ROSS*

Along with Silk Cut and Merit Cup, Toshiba was another, perhaps the, favourite at the start in Southampton. A twenty-four-hour record run as part of their 3,000 mile qualifying voyage just before the start helped, but the real reason was the skipper and crew. Skipper Chris Dickson and navigator Andrew Cape had dominated the previous race, their first, with Tokio – until the mast came down in the fifth leg off Brazil. Watch captain Paul Standbridge had completed four Whitbreads, most notably with second-placed Intrum Justitia in 1993/94. The rest of the crew had four Whitbreads and a great deal of experience in the professional circuits. Dickson stepped down in Cape Town, citing a difference of opinion about the way the project was being run by Team Dennis Conner. Paul Standbridge took over as skipper. Andrew Cape left the boat in Baltimore, and was replaced by Murray Ross.

THE RESULTS

Leg 1

	Yacht	Finish Time	Elapsed Time	Leg Points
1	EF Language	05:54:26 1/10/97	29 16:54:26	125
2	Merit Cup	01:20:11 2/10/98	30 12:20:11	110
3	Innovation Kvaerner	03:09:06 22/10/97	30 14:09:06	97
4	Silk Cut	03:17:00 23/10/98	31 14:17:00	84
5	Chessie Racing	19:12:42 23/10/97	32 06:12:42	72
6	Toshiba	05:23:14 23/10/97	32 16:23:14	60
7	America's Challenge	07:52:38 24/10/97	32 18:52:38	48
8	Swedish Match	14:14:39 24/10/97	33 01:14:39	36
9	EF Education	14:28:02 25/10/97	34 01:28:02	24
10	BrunelSunergy	02:42:54 27/10/97	35 13:42:54	12

Leg 2

	Yacht	Finish Time	Elapsed Time	Leg Pts	Total Pts
1	Swedish Match	15:15:03 23-11-1997	15 03:45:03	125	161
2	Innovation Kvaerner	09:32:35 24-11-1997	15 22:02:35	110	207
3	Toshiba	16:57:12 24-11-1997	16 05:27:12	97	157
4	Silk Cut	02:35:09 25-11-1997	16 15:05:09	84	168
5	EF Language	07:37:25 25-11-1997	16 20:07:25	72	197
6	Chessie Racing	23:21:47 25-11-1997	17 11:51:47	60	132
7	Merit Cup	14:07:47 27-11-1997	19 02:37:47	48	158
8	EF Education	21:45:32 27-11-1997	19 10:15:32	36	60
9	Brunel Sunergy	22:54:39 27-11-1997	19 11:24:39	24	36

Leg 3

	Yacht	Finish Time	Elapsed Time	Leg Pts	Total Pts
1	EF Language	14:39:20 22-12-1997	9 09:09:20	105	302
2	Swedish Match	14:44:28 22-12-1997	9 09:14:28	92	253
3	Chessie Racing	14:45:21 22-12-1997	9 09:15:21	81	213
4	Merit Cup	14:47:37 22-12-1997	9 09:17:37	70	228
5	Innovation Kvaerner	14:49:18 22-12-1997	9 09:19:18	66	267
6	Toshiba	15:00:04 22-12-1997	9 09:30:04	50	207
7	Silk Cut	15:05:01 22-12-1997	9 09:35:01	40	208
8	BrunelSunergy	15:30:04 22-12-1997	9 10:00:04	30	66
9	EF Education	16:18:00 22-12-1997	9 10:48:00	20	80

Leg 4

	Yacht	Finish Time	Elapsed Time	Leg Pts	Total Pts
1	Merit Cup	00:46:08 09-01-1998	4 22:16:08	105	333
2	Toshiba	00:48:44 09-01-1998	4 22:18:44	92	299
3	Chessie Racing	00:58:34 09-01-1998	4 22:28:34	81	294
4	EF Language	01:10:03 09-01-1998	4 22:40:03	70	372
5	Swedish Match	01:27:26 09-01-1998	4 22:57:26	60	313
6	Silk Cut	03:47:37 09-01-1998	5 01:17:37	50	258
7	Innovation Kvaerner	04:28:58 09-01-1998	5 01:58:58	40	307
8	BrunelSunergy	06:34:52 09-01-1998	5 04:04:52	30	96
9	EF Education	08:51:02 09-01-1998	5 06:21:02	20	100

Leg 5

	Yacht	Finish Time	Elapsed Time	Leg Pts	Total Pts
1	EF Language	02:09:23 24-02-1998	23 01:09:23	135	507
2	BrunelSunergy	05:07:17 27-02-1998	26 04:07:17	119	215
3	Chessie Racing	11:31:48 27-02-1998	26 10:31:48	105	399
4	Swedish Match	01:19:09 28-02-1998	27 00:19:09	91	404
5	Merit Cup	02:50:27 28-02-1998	27 01:50:27	78	411
6	Toshiba	03:19:32 28-02-1998	27 02:19:32	0	299
7	Innovation Kvaerner	17:12:15 28-02-1998	27 16:12:15	65	372
8	Silk Cut	03:00:54 03-03-1998	30 02:00:54	26	284
9	EF Education	18:27:00 11-03-1998	38 17:27:00	26	126

Leg 6

	Yacht	Finish Time	Elapsed Time	Leg Pts	Total Pts
1	Silk Cut	13:55:09 23-03-1998	14 19:55:09	115	399
2	EF Language	15:13:17 29-03-1998	14 21:13:17	101	608
3	Swedish Match	17:42:43 29-03-1998	14 23:42:43	89	493
4	Innovation Kvaerner	01:59:07 30-03-1998	15 07:59:07	77	449
5	Merit Cup	05:37:39 30-03-1998	15 11:37:39	66	477
6	Chessie Racing	13:39:12 30-03-1998	15 19:39:12	55	454
7	Toshiba	13:42:05 30-03-1998	15 19:42:05	44	343
8	BrunelSunergy	02:41:35 31-03-1998	16 08:41:35	33	248
9	EF Education	04:40:30 31-03-1998	16 10:40:30	22	148

Leg 7

	Yacht	Finish Time	Elapsed Time	Leg Pts	Total Pts
1	BrunelSunergy	22/04/98 20:59	3 03:59:39	105	353
2	Swedish Match	22/04/98 21:20	3 04:20:24	92	585
3	EF Language	22/04/98 21:20	3 04:20:54	81	689
4	Innovation Kvaerner	22/04/98 21:58	3 04:58:36	70	519
5	Silk Cut	22/04/98 22:02	3 05:02:07	60	459
6	Merit Cup	22/04/98 22:21	3 05:21:44	50	527
7	Toshiba	22/04/98 22:30	3 05:30:43	40	383
8	Chessie Racing	22/04/98 22:30	3 05:30:53	30	484
9	EF Education	22/04/98 22:39	3 05:39:54	20	168

Leg 8

	Yacht	Finish Time	Elapsed Time	Leg Pts	Total Pts
1	Toshiba	16/05/98 17:37	12 23:52:03	115	478
2	Silk Cut	16/05/98 17:47	13 00:02:31	101	560
3	Chessie Racing	16/05/98 20:12	13 02:27:55	89	583
4	EF Education	17/05/98 01:04	13 07:19:57	77	255
5	Merit Cup	17/05/98 01:48	13 08:03:55	66	593
6	EF Language	17/05/98 02:37	13 08:52:16	55	744
7	Swedish Match	17/05/98 05:10	13 11:25:25	44	629
8	Innovation Kvaerner	17/05/98 12:06	13 18:21:31	33	552
9	BrunelSunergy	17/05/98 12:07	13 18:22:41	22	375

Leg 9

	Yacht	Finish Time	Elapsed Time	Leg Pts	Total Pts
1	Merit Cup	24/05/98 11:56	1 22:56:05	105	698
2	EF Language	24/05/98 12:11	1 23:11:37	92	836
3	Innovation Kvaerner	24/05/98 12:21	1 23:21:22	81	633
4	Silk Cut	24/05/98 12:31	1 23:31:41	70	630
5	Swedish Match	24/05/98 12:51	1 23:51:18	60	689
6	Toshiba	24/05/98 12:56	1 23:56:27	50	528
7	BrunelSunergy	24/05/98 12:57	1 23:57:35	40	415
8	Chessie Racing	24/05/98 14:22	2 01:22:24	30	613
9	EF Education	24/05/98 15:22	2 02:22:14	20	275

TEAM EF BUSINESS PARTNERS

SONY NORDIC   POSTGIROT   SUN MICROSYSTEMS

DAGENS INDUSTRI   SEMCON   PEAK PERFORMANCE   MTV PRODUKTION

RENAULT, HANSER PRODUKTION, AWLGRIP, SECUMAR, QUALITY HOTEL 11, ERIKSBERGS FÖRVALTNINGS AB,

BOSTADSBOLAGET I GÖTEBORG AB, ROBLON, ROCKPORT, ADVOKATFIRMAN GLIMSTEDT, PROLABBET, TROSA TRYCKERI, COMVIQ, SIEMENS, IMS DATA,

STJÄRNAFYRKANT INTERNATIONAL, COOL CARRIERS, SKANSKA, SCA GRAPHICS

PRODUCT SUPPLIERS: LINJEPUNKT, RUTER PRESS, CARL LAMM, REVO SUNGLASSES, AB PRIPPS BRYGGERIER, BUCK TOOLS,

EFFEKT POWER BARS, SVENSKA ÖRTMEDICINSKA INSTITUTET

BOATYARD PARTNERS BUILDING EF LANGUAGE AND EF EDUCATION IN GOTHENBURG:

AMU, ARBETSFÖRMEDLINGEN, ARGUS, BEIJERS, BLÅKLÄDER, BORÉNS BRAND, BRÖDERNA EDSTRAND, BULTEN STAINLESS, CARL LIDÉN, CRAWFORD,

ESSVE PRODUKTER, FESTO, GÖTEBORG TRÄ & FANÉR, GOTIA FASTENINGS AB, GYCOM, GÖTEBORG FRITID, GÖTEBORGS MOBIL KRANAR, INTERN TELE AB,

KAMEWA AB, KONTIKAB, LUNDBY KROG, MCR, MUNTERS, PIAB, RAYCHEM, RENHÅLLNINGSVERKET, SJÖGRENS, SKOGLUNDS ÅKERI, SMIDESBOLAGET,

SOS ALARM, KARL STORZ ENDOSKOP, TEGMA AB, THELANDER & ALMKVIST, TIDERMANS, TOPCON OPTICAL SVENSKA,

TWINS ELOXERING, WIRATOR

PHOTO CREDITS: ALL PICTURES BY RICK TOMLINSON ARE SHOT WITH NIKON CAMERAS ON FUJI FILM.

THE PICTURES IN THE BOOK ARE ALL TAKEN BY RICK TOMLINSON EXCEPT THE FOLLOWING:

THIERRY MARTINEZ: 86, 94-95, 98-99, 100, 103, 108-109, 146, 147, 186-187, 206-207, 208, 209, 210, 215, 216-217

LEAH NEWBOLD: 51, 52 (LEFT), 53 (LEFT), 59, 62, 63, 64-65, 115, 116, 117, 118, 120-121, 122-123, 148, 151, 185, 188-189, 192-193, 213, 214 (LEFT)

JUSTIN CLOUGHER: 32, 35 (RIGHT), 37, 42-43, 44, 82, 83, 90, 91, 130, 138-139, 142-143, 144-145, 169, 171, 197, 198, 202-203

JOHAN SALÉN: 126, 127, 128-129, 199 MARK PEPPER: 214 (RIGHT), 218 (BOTTOM)

MIKE HEWITT, ALLSPORT: 46-47 STEPHEN MUNDAY, ALLSPORT: 97

THE BOOK IS PRINTED ON ENVIRONMENTALLY SUITABLE PAPER, 150 GRAM SILVERBLADE, TCF, FROM SILVERDALEN, SWEDEN.